TO
GIVE
LIFE

TO GIVE LIFE

The UJA
in the Shaping
of the American
Jewish Community

ABRAHAM J. KARP

SCHOCKEN BOOKS New York

First published by Schocken Books 1981
10 9 8 7 6 5 4 3 2 1   81 82 83

Library of Congress Cataloging in Publication Data

Karp, Abraham J
  To give life.

  Bibliography: p.
  Includes index.
  1. United Jewish Appeal. 2. Jews in the United
States—Politics and government. I. Title.
HV3191.K37   362.8'4924'06073   80–16487

Manufactured in the United States of America
ISBN 0–8052–3751–8

Acknowledgements

The author gratefully acknowledges the interest and help of Professor Moshe Davis, founding director of the Institute of Contemporary Jewry, the Hebrew University, Jerusalem; and Irving Bernstein and Eve Weiss of the United Jewish Appeal. I am particularly beholden to David Mark, a gifted writer and sensitive editor.

Special thanks go to Murray H. Goodman for his generous support, and to Michael L. Klein, Dr. Robert A. Rubenstein, Herbert J. Solomon, and Sherman H. Starr for their help in making publication of this book possible.

For
Rabbi Philip S. Bernstein
actor in the drama of
a remnant saved and
a nation reborn

Contents

Prologue   ix

Introduction   xi

I. TOWARD UNITY

1. The Sense of Community   3
2. A Community Organizes   9
3. A Position of Parity   15
4. The Perception of Power   23
5. Democracy from Above: Congress and Conference   31

II. TO AID A BROTHER

6. "That They May Not Hunger and Perish"   39
7. "Appeal to Their Brethren in America"   45
8. "Enduring Cooperation on Behalf of Jewish Causes"   59
9. "A Lasting and Permanent Unity"   65

III. WE ARE ONE

10. The United Jewish Appeal: Beginnings   77
11. 1946: A Year of Testing and Triumph   87
12. Eyes Toward Zion   93
13. 1947–1950: Years of Rescue and Return   99

14. In and with the Communities   109
15. At the Tercentenary and Beyond   117
16. Confrontation and Cooperation   123
17. Leadership from the Community   137
18. The Summer of 1967 and the Fall of 1973   145
19. The United Jewish Appeal at Forty   159
20. This Spring in Jerusalem   173
21. Epilogue: On a Personal Note   187

    Bibliographical Notes   189
    Index   197

Prologue

The ballroom was filled with men and women high in the ranks of leadership in the American Jewish community. They had gathered for the National Leadership Dinner which opened the annual conference of the United Jewish Appeal celebrating its fortieth anniversary, December 7, 1978.

Here and there one recognized a familiar face, seen on the dais at a rally in 1948, or heard at a meeting in 1967, or met on a mission in 1973. New faces outnumbered them.

At each table were *kippot* and *Birkhat Hamazon* (Grace after Meals) booklets. Some of those present wore skullcaps as a matter of course; others put them on as a mark of identity. A blessing preceded the meal and Grace concluded it. In the recital of the benedictions there were those who chanted them by heart, others who followed the Hebrew or the English. Many sat in respectful silence.

Simcha Dinitz, Israel's ambassador to Washington, completing an eventful tour of duty, bade an affectionate and challenging farewell to the assembled American Jewish leaders.

Baron Guy de Rothschild, head of Jewry's premier family, offered the gratitude of his own community—French Jewry, now grown to fourth largest in the world—for brotherly concern and aid, for having given, and for having taught others how to organize the enterprise of giving. One sensed a transferring of the mantle of generosity from the shoulders of the elite of European Jewry to those organized for generosity in the American Jewish community.

The chairman, Irwin S. Field, a young man grown up in UJA service and leadership, proceeded to what has become the central ritual at fundraising dinners, the calling of pledge cards. Sums were announced in tones of gratitude and duty. Shades of pronunciation indicated a diversity of background. Some elders spoke with an eastern European accent or a western European intonation. In others one heard unmistakable New Yorkese, the twang of the Midwest, or the drawl of the South. The atmosphere was one of solemnity made warm and familial by the geniality and grace of the chairman.

When all prepared cards had been called, the chairman asked whether anyone else cared to come forth. A few more rose to announce their pledges. The last to speak did so in the marked accent of an immigrant from eastern Europe:

> Mr. Chairman, in 1939 they took us to the camps. In 1949 the Joint brought me to America, the Bronx. It was before Pesach. On the holiday I went to *shul*. Before *Yizkor*, they had an appeal for the UJA. People were pledging, a thousand, five thousand, ten thousand dollars. I also pledged. I pledged two dollars. My salary was fifteen dollars a week. Mr Chairman, it is my great privilege to announce my pledge for this year: twenty-five thousand dollars.

Introduction

The story of the Jew in America begins with an act of brotherly concern, one Jewish community's coming to the aid of another. The twenty-three Jewish refugees from Portuguese-occupied Brazil who found asylum in New Amsterdam in late summer 1654 were threatened with expulsion. Gov. Peter Stuyvesant urged the Dutch West India Company to permit him to send them on their way. When news of their plight reached the mother city of Amsterdam, leading Jews of that community interceded in their behalf. Plea and persuasion availed and the American Jewish community came into being.

The history of the Jew in America can be traced as a repayment for this act of brotherly concern, as an ongoing and growing commitment to the well-being of the Jewish communities of the Old World by those of the New.

The record of American Jewry's coming to the aid of European, Asian, and African Jewish communities has largely been documented. It is a saga of concern, persistence, skill, and great generosity. A glowing chapter is being added by the present generation.

It would be of interest and importance to consider what that exercise of persuasion and generosity has done to and for the

American Jewish community. In this essay we shall attempt to indicate some benefits which have accrued to the organized life of that community from its excursions into two aspects of that endeavor: political persuasion and philanthropy. We shall deal with an era of one hundred forty years, 1840–1979, which has been the effective life span of American Jewry as a self-conscious community. The concentration will be on the effects of political efforts in the first eighty years, 1840–1920, and philanthropic endeavors in the six decades which followed.

I
TOWARD UNITY

The feeling was universal among them that united action was imperatively needed. . . . First, to take steps to the end that these barbarities might cease and never recur; second, that material help be promptly extended.

> —Response to Kishinev Pogrom, 1905,
> from the Ninth Annual Report of
> the American Jewish Committee,
> *American Jewish Year Book*
> (5677, 1916–1917), p. 324

1.

The Sense of Community

Secretary of State John Forsyth received a communiqué from the American consular representative in Syria, a Macedonian named Jasper Chasseaud, dated March 24, 1840. He reported:

> On the 5th of February last the Revd Capouchin Thomas, president of the Catholic Church of Damascus . . . disappeared from that city. . . . The Jew Barber was questioned, taken into prison, and after the application of some torments to his person he confessed that the Revd Thomas had been beheaded . . . by seven of his coreligioners of Damascus . . . in order to take his Blood, it being ordered by their religion to make use of Christian Blood in their Unleavened Bread at Easter.
>
> The seven Jews thus accused . . . 64 children, belonging to those families . . . were immediately taken into prison, and after severe tortures and threats several of them confessed. . . . The inquisition of the Jews in the city . . . continues with much vigor and no Jew can show his face out in the streets.

The unfortunate Jews of Damascus were victims of the medieval European blood libel accusation now come to the Near East. They were caught in the vise of an international conflict between the viceroy of Egypt sponsored by France and the Turkish sultan backed by England. The French consul in

Damascus promoted the accusation, exploiting the incident for French imperialist interests.

The world press turned its attention to the "affair." For reasons humanitarian and political, the hue and cry against the "outrage" was most pronounced in Great Britain. The newly emancipated Jewries of western Europe reacted with all vigor. The Rothschilds in France and Austria exerted their not inconsequential influence. Because of favorable public opinion and positive governmental interest, English Jewry took the lead.

Sir Moses Montefiore took up his position as champion of his oppressed brethren. With the solid backing of the Jewish Board of Deputies, he set out to Egypt, accompanied by Isaac Crémieux, representing French Jewry. The protests, prayers, and pleas of an aroused European Jewry went with them in what turned out to be a successful mission.

The traditional Jewish sentiments of oneness and shared fate impelled the Jews of the world to act in defense of their persecuted brethren. In 1840, they did so, but with the sense of at long last entering the stage of world history as actors "speaking their own lines." The Rothschilds, Montefiore, Crémieux, spoke for a people beginning to forge its own destiny. The contention of Joseph Jacobs that modern Jewish history dates from the Damascus Affair is an astute one.

It can be argued that the American Jewish community had its beginnings as a self-conscious entity in the activity precipitated by "the massacre of Damascus." When the news reached these shores, American Jewry moved with vigor and boldness. Meetings were held in every community and resolutions demanded intercession by the government.

The Jews of New York wrote President Van Buren: "We beg leave to express what we are persuaded is the unanimous opinion of the Israelites throughout the Union, that you will cheerfully use every possible effort to induce the Pascha of Egypt to manifest more liberal treatment towards his Jewish subjects . . . ."

PERSECUTION

OF

THE JEWS IN THE EAST.

CONTAINING THE

PROCEEDINGS OF A MEETING

HELD AT

THE SYNAGOGUE MIKVEH ISRAEL, PHILADELPHIA,

ON THURSDAY EVENING, THE 28th OF AB, 5600.

CORRESPONDING WITH

THE 27th OF AUGUST, 1840.

———————

PHILADELPHIA:

C. SHERMAN & CO. PRINTERS, 19 ST. JAMES STREET.

1840.

5

The Israelites of Charleston addressed the president of the United States "with a request that [these resolutions] be sent to the Resident Ministers of Foreign Courts in the United States." They also appointed a committee of five "to confer with the Richmond Committee, and others." Richmond Jewry in turn was already thanking "the Chief Magistrate of this Great Republic," and acting "in common with brethren . . . elsewhere."

These then are expressions of Jewish concern for the plight of brethren overseas by Jews so at home in America as to feel free to petition their government to act in their interests, as they conceived their interests to be. Theirs also was the wisdom to phrase their concerns in language expressing broad humanitarian principles. Above all, we find evidence of a sense of national Jewish communal unity, a unity which enabled the Jews of New York to speak of "the unanimous opinion of the Israelites throughout the Union," which urged the Jews of Charleston "to confer with the Richmond Committee," and the Richmond community to feel that they hold interests "in common with brethren . . . elsewhere."

All these sentiments were expressed at the meetings held in Philadelphia. The *Pennsylvania Inquirer and Daily Courier* devoted fully two-thirds of its news page to it, and the account of the meeting was published as a pamphlet. A committee of correspondence was appointed "to correspond with other Committees in their country," and it framed a letter to the president expressing the sentiments of the "Jewish inhabitants of Philadelphia . . . in conjunction with our brethren of other cities."

The tragic event in far-off Damascus evoked dormant sentiments of kinship and oneness, not only with suffering brethren abroad, but also with Jewish residents in other American communities. It caused American Jewry to realize that, dispersed as it was throughout the entire land, and organized as it was in a variety of congregations, it was one community in faith, sentiments, and destiny.

Isaac Leeser, Hazzan-minister of Philadelphia's Mikveh Israel congregation, spoke of Jewish unity and responsibility: "As citizens, we belong to the country we live in. . . . as inheritors of the Law, the Jews of England, and Russia, and Sweden, are no aliens among us. . . . oceans may intervene between our dispersed remnants . . . but, the Israelite is ever alive to the welfare of his distant brother."

Moreover, he recognized that this concern for the welfare of distant brothers united the Jews of America. Seizing upon this perceived unity, he attempted a year later to form a union of American Israelites. Under his guidance a circular signed by representatives of "the Sephardim . . . the Ashkenazim and of the Polish synagogues" was circulated. It contained detailed plans for the union, and urged the convening of a .founding conference. As he later wrote, "the conference did not meet. . . . no union was established . . . and the incipient division and party strife were permitted to take what shape they pleased."

He attributed the failure to the opposition of the Sephardi grandees ruling New York's Shearith Israel congregation, who feared that the proposed union would be dominated by the numerically superior German Jews. But the sense of unity of the national community initiated by the response to the Damascus Affair persisted. In agreement or dissent, in concerted action or intramural strife, after 1840 American Jewry knew itself to be *one* community.

2.

A Community Organizes

In the two decades which followed, the Jewish community increased tenfold to reach one hundred fifty thousand in 1860. Mass immigration from the German states had increased the community in numbers and diversity. Reform temples were organized in New York and Baltimore in the 1840s, and in the 1850s the pattern of traditional congregations turning Reform became established. The spokesman for the Traditionalists, Leeser's *The Occident,* began publication in 1843. A decade later it was joined by the moderate Reform weekly *The Israelite,* edited by Isaac Mayer Wise, and David Einhorn's Radical Reform *Sinai.* Diversity in religious ways and views filled their pages. The antagonists were not above labeling each other "Haman," "malicious slanderer," "ignoramus of the first water," and "Russian serf." An attempt to bring a degree of unity into the internal life of American Jewry, at a conference convened in Cleveland in 1855, quickly and dramatically disclosed that the community was even more splintered than had been suspected.

Although the community was sundered by differences in faith, it could still join in a shared concern about Jewish fate. The cause which aroused the Jews of America in the 1850s was a

proposed treaty of peace between the United States and Switzerland which would not have adequately protected the rights of
Jewish citizens of the United States visiting in Switzerland.
Leeser, Wise, and Einhorn could pause in the heat of the battles
fought in "the wars of the Lord" to take up arms against a
common enemy. It was not lost upon leaders of American Jewry
that a united community would be more effective in its protests
and petitions. But internal disunity remained and was
intensified by an ever-increasing immigration which lent ethnic
diversity to religious division. Only a crisis of dramatic intensity would bring on communal unity which would bridge the
diversities.

On the morning of June 24, 1858, the parents of six-year-old
Edgardo Mortara of Bologna, Italy, found their son missing.
They soon learned that he had been abducted by the Papal
Guards and had been placed in a monastery in Rome. Five years
earlier a Catholic servant in the Mortara household had secretly
baptized little Edgardo. She thought he was about to die and
wanted to "save" his eternal soul. When she confessed to her
priest what she had done, he informed the papal authorities,
who proceeded to remove the baptized Catholic child from the
Judaizing influences of his parents. The Mortara family fought
valiantly to regain their son, but to no avail. The pope remained
adamant, even in the face of an international outcry against this
"heartless act." Napoleon II, guardian of the Holy See, issued
words of protest and warning. German rabbis sent a petition,
Sir Moses Montefiore sought an audience, mass meetings de-
cried papal obstinacy, but Pope Pius IX remained obstinate. The
baptism of the child had made him a Christian, and neither
parental tears nor public cry of outrage could alter his condition.

At mass meetings held in New York, San Francisco, and other
major American cities, Jew and Gentile joined in condemning
the deed and in pleading for its annulment. The mass meetings
were accompanied by editorials and newspaper articles, and
even the muses of drama and poetry were invoked to denounce
papal power and condemn Catholic intransigence.

The youthful American Jewish community, flexing its developing communal muscles, jumped into the fray. A sense of common outrage united the disparate "ethnic" components and the differing religious movements and set them working together in shared concern and enterprise. The Sephardi, German, Polish, Russian, Dutch, English, and French communities found each other and discovered that they had much in common. Traditionalists and Reformers discovered that while doctrinal differences may divide a community, an awareness of a shared destiny can unite it, and that the welfare of brethren demanded such unity.

A number of leading American Jews, notably the Rev. Samuel M. Isaacs, rabbi of Congregation Shaarey Tefillah of New York and editor of the *Jewish Messenger*, argued that if the American Jewish community had been formally united, it would have been far more effective in its attempts to secure American governmental intervention in the affair. Leeser reported that "Ever since the Mortara meeting at New York, some of the leading men have labored in getting up a Board."

The "Board of Delegates of American Israelites" was established at the end of 1859 by representatives of twenty-five congregations. Leeser's description was an exaggeration born of approval: "a comparative numerous body, representing twenty-five various communities of the country." Actually, the twenty-five congregations represented no more than ten cities on the eastern seaboard and New Orleans, and all the founding congregations were in the Traditionalist camp. A decade later membership was extended "to every incorporated society of Israelites."

Despite the pleas of Leeser for an organization which would deal with all aspects of the internal life of American Jewry, the organizers felt it prudent to limit its projected activities to:

1. Keeping a watchful eye on all occurrences at home and abroad
2. Collecting statistics
3. Aiding religious education

The last mentioned was found to be too much of an intrusion on the absolute autonomy of the congregations and was changed to: "To promote and encourage education among the Israelites in the Orient." That its field of legitimate interest focused primarily on matters abroad can be seen from an objective added later:

4. To keep up communication with similar central Israelitish bodies throughout the world, and in time, to establish a thorough union among all the Israelites of the United States.

As one reads this objective in the context of the entire constitution, one perceives that the proposed "thorough union" is for matters of external relations rather than domestic activity. It was recognized that the American Jewish community of the time (the 1870s) was marked by a unity in diversity: a unity brought about by and directed toward the situation of Jews abroad, and a diversity which marked their life at home.

Thus, as one of its first acts, it called the attention of American Jews to the "Appalling Destruction of the Morocco Refugees" in 1859, and acted as the fundraising organization; and one of its last annual reports (1874) deals mainly with its labors in behalf of Roumanian Jewry, the Jews of Persia, and the Jews of Palestine. Its efforts internally were devoted to gathering statistics and Jewish "defense," although it did aid in the establishment of Maimonides College, the first Jewish seminary in America, and in the reestablishment of the Jewish Publication Society, both short-lived enterprises.

The growing Reform movement at first actively opposed, and later just remained aloof from, the board. Ironically, the board became absorbed in the Union of American Hebrew Congregations, and what began as a Traditionalist organization to "establish a thorough union among all the Israelites of the United States" ended as a committee in the Union of Reform Congregations.

THE

JEWS IN ROUMANIA:

THEIR RECENT PERSECUTIONS; MEASURES FOR THEIR PROTECTION.

———

New York:

JOSEPH DAVIS, PRINTER, 645 BROADWAY.

5632–1872.

Its founding demonstrated that the underlying unity in the American Jewish community surfaces when it is challenged to respond to a crisis situation abroad. Its activities, fashioned to confront the challenge, indicated the need for an organization institutionalizing that unity, so that the concerns of the community can receive forceful expression and the united community can exert effective influence. We can also note that the organization born out of the unity fostered by an external crisis can be used to address internal needs and projects.

The response to the Damascus Affair gave to American Jewry its sense of community; the Mortara Affair brought forth the first institutionalization of that perception.

3.

A Position of Parity

The bomb which took the life of Alexander II, "czar of all the Russias," in March 1881 set in motion events that radically altered the American Jewish community. Pogroms in more than one hundred cities followed the assassination. Restrictive laws aimed at the elimination of the Jew from economic and civic life were enacted. Political and economic oppression caused a wave of emigration which in the next half century brought to the United States over two and a half million eastern European Jews, ten times as many as resided here at the beginning of this era.

The quarter of a million Jews who comprised the community in 1880 were mainly immigrants or the children of immigrants from the German states. They were becoming rapidly integrated into the larger social and economic community, and were neither ready nor willing to welcome a mass of Jewish immigrants from Russia which almost doubled their number in the first decade and doubled it again in the next. A spokesman for the United Jewish Charities of Rochester expressed the sentiments of many, calling the Russian Jews "a bane to the country and a curse to all Jews."

It was the Jews of western Europe who first came to the aid of the Jewish immigrants. Their main motivation was no doubt to aid brethren in distress, but self-interest played its role as well. The Jews of Germany, France, and England organized the migration from the towns and cities of Russia to the port cities of France and England where the refugees boarded ships for the New World. The Alliance Israelite helped the immigrant leave his native land. The journey across Europe was the responsibility of the German Central Committee. The London Manor House Committee undertook to help get the immigrant to his final destination—America. The Jewish communities of western Europe preferred to serve as conduit and bridge rather than as place of final residence.

Organized American Jewry did extend aid to the newcomer, albeit with reluctance. The Board of Delegates, the Russian Emigrant Relief Fund, and the Hebrew Emigrant Aid Society, while helping those who arrived, advocated that the immigration be selective and controlled. "It was understood that you were to send us only the strong and able-bodied, willing to work and possessing a knowledge of some handicraft," the Relief Committee complained in a letter to the Alliance.

One perceives a picture of a bewildered and overwhelmed American Jewish community in the early 1880s. It was bewildered by the threat posed to its status by the influx of Russian Jews, coreligionists to be sure, but differing from the resident Jew in dress, speech, religion, education, and the refinements of civilization. Overwhelmed by the magnitude of the problem descending upon it, it looked to European Jewry for direction and aid. Moritz Ellinger, sent to Europe by the Hebrew Emigrant Aid Society in 1882, was "directed to ask the advice and suggestions of the European Committees as to methods of operation" and to "obtain aid from all Hebrews wherever resident." The advice was forthcoming, and the aid as well. Some $112,000 was sent by the European committees to these shores. The American Jewish community dared not as yet present itself as an equal to the older and more firmly established communities of western Europe. It considered them more stable, better integrated, more secure in their status than American Jews, who had enjoyed civic rights and political equality for a far longer period than the Jews of the "free countries" of the Old World.

A decade later the perception and mood had altered. *An Appeal* by the American Committee for Ameliorating the Condition of the Russian Refugees was issued on October 20, 1891. It states that "For the past ten years thousands of our brethren in faith have sought refuge in our country." No longer are they disdained by the "native element." Their spirit is compared to the "resolute determination that animated the Pilgrim Fathers," with the boast that "thousands have become useful citizens." And those who now come "do not come in quest of charity; they come not as paupers seeking alms; they come in search of means to subsist by their own efforts." The committee is also certain that "the people of the United States ever in sympathy with the oppressed of all nations who come to our shores . . . will stand by us in our exertions." It suggests that providing aid to immigrant brethren is not only a demand of the Jewish tradition but also a mandate from the American ethos. It urges participation in the "local societies now forming in every city, town and village in this country."

Two American delegates attended a conference called by the European agencies in Berlin on October 21–22, 1891. Dr. Julius Goldman of the United Hebrew Charities proposed a sharing of financial responsibilities by the American and European societies. The Europeans accepted his offer and authorized an agreement with their American counterparts. American Jewry had now achieved parity with the Jewish communities of western Europe. This elevation of status spurred American Jewry to unite in a Central Refugee Committee comprised of representatives of the Baron de Hirsch Fund, the Russian Transportation Fund, the United Hebrew Charities, and the American Committee for Ameliorating the Condition of the Russian Exiles. This last group had been founded at a meeting which was attended not only by the above, but also by delegates

The American Committee
For Ameliorating the Condition of Russian Refugees.

EXECUTIVE OFFICES, 45 BROADWAY, ROOM 89.

NEW YORK, October 20, 1891.

AN APPEAL.

For the past ten years thousands of our brethren in faith have sought refuge in our country from the relentless persecution of a despotic government, which drove them from the homes where their fathers had dwelled, and where stood the cradles of their infants.

They knew the hardships which awaited them in a new country in which a language is spoken unfamiliar to their ears, and where customs prevail in utter variance with those of the country whence they came.

With the same resolute determination that animated the Pilgrim Fathers when they landed in a world that knew not the tread of the white man, they steeled themselves with courage to overcome all difficulties, to shrink from no task that might be required of them, in order to build for themselves and their families peaceful homes in the glorious land of freedom and religious liberty.

Many possessed skill and accomplishments in various handicrafts and in agriculture, and they had only to become conversant with the changed mode of labor to find remunerative employment, or start out in some occupation on their own account.

Thus thousands have become useful and respected citizens, living in comfort with their families, and contributing thereby in no small degree to dispel the cruel prejudice as to their characters and pursuits, which their enemies strove insidiously to disseminate.

As long as the stream of immigration was confined within moderate limits, the arrangements for extending the needed help to the new comers proved sufficient.

Now, however, when, owing to increased virulence and persistence of inhuman oppression and persecution, the rush of immigration has become overwhelming, the means and methods heretofore resorted to, even with the aid of the generous provision made by the great philanthropist, Baron de Hirsch, have become totally inadequate to the needs of the hour.

It is our plain duty, inspired by religion and love of humanity, and by loyalty to our country, to extend a helping hand and render every support towards self-dependence to the innocent victims of rapine and bigotry.

18

They do not come in quest of charity ; they come not as paupers, seeking alms ; they come in search of means to subsist by their own efforts, under the favorable conditions which our country offers to every honest toiler and worker. Nor is there any lack of opportunity. Our country is large and wide enough, and has employment for all who are willing to labor.

The problem which presents itself is to find proper fields wherein the immigrants can procure the work they are in search of, and they are fitted for the varied handicrafts and agricultural pursuits. They must not be allowed to crowd special localities, but should be dispersed over the whole land. Thus they will be easily absorbed, and, what is all important, will become Americanized more readily, and in less time than if permitted to aggregate in a few large cities.

The people of the United States, ever in sympathy with the oppressed of all nations who come to our shores with the determination of securing an honorable existence by their own efforts, will stand by us in our exertions for the aid and relief of our unfortunate brethren. We may also feel confident that the public authorities, as far as it lies within their power, will assist us in a task, which, in its result, will prove a benefit to the whole country by enriching it with the product of the labor of honest and useful citizens.

Let us, then, go to work, singly and unitedly, with warm hearts and cheerful willingness, young and old, rich and poor ; let each contribute according to his means ; *let each and every one strive to find employment, to find a home for at least one family.* The opportunity is given to assist in this philanthropic work by taking part in the formation of local societies now forming in every city, town and village in the country. Remember that a heavy responsibility rests upon us all alike, and we must be ready to assume our share of the burden.

LEWIS SEASONGOOD, Cincinnati, O., President.
LAZARUS SILVERMAN, Chicago, } Vice-Pres.
JOSEPH FOX, New York. }
JACOB H. SCHIFF, New York, Treasurer.
ADOLPHUS S. SOLOMONS, Washington, D.C. } Secs.
BERNARD HARRIS, Philadelphia. }

Executive Committee.

M. WARLEY PLATZEK, New York, Chairman.   JULIUS FREIBERG, Cincinnati, Vice-Chairman.

JULIUS BIEN, New York.	AARON HAAS, Atlanta, Ga.	SOLOMON LOEB, New York.
MARCUS BERNHEIMER, St. Louis.	ISAAC HAMBURGER, New York.	ELIAS LOWENSTEIN, Memphis, Tenn.
MARTIN BUTZEL, Detroit.	JACOB H. HECHT, Boston, Mass.	ADOLPH LOEB, Chicago, Ill.
EMANUEL COHEN, Minneapolis, Minn.	MYER S. ISAACS, New York.	SIMON MUHR, Philadelphia, Pa.
DAVID SOLIS COHEN, Portland, Ore.	LEO N. LEVI, Galveston, Texas.	HENRY RICE, New York.
AARON FRIEDENWALD, Baltimore, Md.	FERDINAND LEVY, New York.	JULIUS ROSENTHAL, Chicago, Ill.
BERNARD GROSS, Milwaukee, Wisc.	LOUIS E. LEVY, Philadelphia, Pa.	SIMON WOLF, Washington, D.C.
	MORRIS TUSKA, New York.	SAMUEL WOOLNER, Peoria, Ill.

19

from the Independent Order of B'nai B'rith, the Free Sons of Israel, the Union of American Hebrew Congregations, and the Jewish Alliance of America. The participation of the Jewish Alliance is most significant. It had been called into being by a "group of American Jews of Russian origin" who invited "other American Jews chiefly of German origin . . . to join."

Russian Jewish immigrants were among the first to organize aid for the new arrivals. As early as 1885 they had organized the Association of Jewish Immigrants of Philadelphia, which did important work in welcoming immigrants to these shores and seeing them to their final destinations. It became the model for other such enterprises which followed. In immigrant aid activities German and Russian Jews met and first began to learn to work together. Although it was to be a long time before the communities became united, the seeds were laid in the immigrant aid societies.

During the decade 1880–1890, there was an intensification both in the diversity and the unity of the American Jewish community. The immigrant tide transformed the community, tipping the numerical balance to the eastern European Jews. However, the German Jews retained the power which wealth and status confer. Thus the communities were divided socially, economically, and religiously. The fraternal orders, B'nai B'rith chief among them, did not welcome Russian Jews. Socially, the communities remained apart and separate. Religious divisions became institutionalized in the middle of the decade. Nineteen Reform rabbis met in Pittsburgh, spelling out a Judaism bereft of ritual and antagonistic to Jewish national sentiments, which would keep their temples free of eastern European immigrant Jews. A year later acculturated Traditionalists and moderate Reformers established the Jewish Theological Seminary, whose rabbis would have great appeal to the children of the immigrants but little to the immigrants themselves. In the next year New York's Orthodox Jews organized and brought Rabbi Jacob Joseph of Vilna as their chief rabbi to give institutional viability to their concept of Judaism. The concretization of

American religious Jewry into the tripartite division which obtains to the present dates back to this decisive decade.

It was primarily in immigrant aid work that German and Russian Jews met in communal endeavor. They were often in confrontation, but commitment to the cause brought forth ever-growing cooperation. Immigrant aid work also linked American Jewry with the Jews of western Europe in joint enterprise. At first it was the adolescent, seeking the guidance and aid of the adults. But the press of events in this decisive decade provided rapid maturation for American Jewry which raised it to a status of equality with the older and more organized communities of the Old World.

The Damascus Affair evoked the sense of community. The Mortara Affair pointed to the need for communal organization. The "decisive decade" catapulted the organized American Jewish community to the status of parity with the leading Jewish communities of the world.

4.

The Perception of Power

Late in October of 1899, the Lower East Side of New York was flooded with election handbills in Yiddish. They urged Jews to vote for Theodore Roosevelt for governor of the State of New York, and were issued by "Jewish Members of the Republican State Committee." The appeal was directed to Jewish ethnic interests and emotions: How can a Jew vote against the man who was so instrumental in helping bring Spain to its knees in the Spanish-American War? It reminded the reader of the Inquisition and the fires of the auto-da-fé. At long last "Spain now lies punished for all her sins." This was accomplished by "the Republican Party through its president . . . and the Republican gubernatorial candidate, Theodore Roosevelt. . . . Every vote for the Colonel of the Rough Riders is approval of McKinley and the War. Every vote for Roosevelt's opponent is a vote for Spain. . . . Vote to express your approval of Spain's defeat."

It is a strange and instructive document. It suggests that in the perception of the Jewish members of the Republican State Committee, events which occurred centuries ago across the Atlantic, and in their century in the Caribbean, were more powerful in determining the attitude of the Jewish immigrant than events in his own state or city or neighborhood. It was based on the recognition that the vote provided political power, and that the "ethnics" voted their own parochial interests and sentiments. It implied that it was legitimate to vote in response to one's ethnic self-interest. It spoke a reality of American political life: groups will cast their vote on a single issue, if that issue is perceived as touching upon the security and/or status of the group, or addresses itself to something which stirs deep group emotions.

The Jews in America at the turn of the century numbered over a million, and more were sure to come. In New York City they already constituted a significant voting bloc. Because of the importance of bloc votes in the Electoral College scheme of choosing a president, the concentration of Jewish votes in the largest states would give them political power beyond their numbers. The Jewish community had already petitioned the government on issues touching Jewish well-being: the Swiss Treaty, Order #11, the Russian Treaty, the condition of Jews in Roumania, the proposed "Christian Nation" amendment to the Constitution, and the Damascus and Mortara Affairs, among others. It had done so through ad hoc committees which had rallied public opinion and made representation to governmental authorities. In the latter part of the century a Washington lawyer and sometime government official, Simon Wolf, served as the unofficial yet accepted Jewish lobbyist in the national capital. Would it not be far more effective if there were an organization representing the Jewish community and active in its behalf in matters touching its welfare?

The reasons for establishing such a body seemed compelling to the leaders of the Jewish establishment, the financiers, merchant princes, and lawyers who had assumed a *noblesse oblige* responsibility for Jewish well-being at home and abroad. The Jewish situation in the Russian empire was growing constantly more ominous; racism was expressing itself through anti-Semitism in Germany; France, the land of "liberty, equality, and fraternity," had disclosed its latent anti-Semitism in the Dreyfus case. At home, the immigrant mass was creating social problems and group tensions, and an increasing immigrant population would heighten these. The immigrant Jews were beginning to show political awareness and some were already engaged in radical social and economic activities. The eastern European Jews at the turn of the century outnumbered the German Jews four to one, and the ratio was rapidly increasing. If their leaders were to speak for American Jewry they would no doubt do so in a manner which would not be conducive to securing the status and influence of the Jewish community. In a word, the time had arrived for the "prudent element" of American Jewry to formalize and institutionalize the leadership which it had assumed and which it was now exerting.

There was a twofold problem which urged caution and made for delay. Such an organization must not be viewed by the general community as a "government within a government," raising suspicions of divided political loyalties; it should not be viewed as a self-serving ethnic pressure group. Its activities should not "embarrass" the democratic process in which Americans engage as citizens, rather than as members of subgroups; a new quasi-political ethnic body would imply the inadequacy of the existing political set-up. It also would need, at the very least, the acceptance of the larger segment of the Jewish community, the eastern European Jews who would not be represented in the composition and deliberations of this body.

Clearly what was needed was a cause which would bring about the organization of such a body, but which would be of such universal humanitarian appeal as to offset the fears outlined above, and win the approval of that larger Jewish community.

The Kishinev Pogroms in 1903 and 1905, and other pogroms which erupted in czarist domains in 1905 and 1906, provided the cause and created the mandate. The pogrom on Easter 1903 took the lives of forty-nine Jews, wounded some five hundred more, looted seven hundred homes, and destroyed six hundred business establishments. Russians and Roumanians, townspeople and peasants, joined in the murder and looting. Students, including those studying for the priesthood, played a leading role, while the four thousand soldiers stationed in the city stood by. The pogrom, prepared for by anti-Semitic newspaper articles, was touched off by a blood libel accusation and orchestrated by local governmental authorities. Overnight "Kishinev" became the catchword for anti-Jewish excesses viewed benignly by the czarist government.

Protest meetings were held in major cities of the world. The reaction to the outrage was particularly strong in the United States. A petition of protest was presented to President Theodore Roosevelt to be delivered to the czar, but the Russian government refused to accept it. Indignation was added to outrage. Committees were formed to aid the victims, who increased in number in the next two years, climaxed by another pogrom in Kishinev in August 1905. The Ninth Annual Report of the American Jewish Committee, published in the *American Jewish Year Book* (5677, 1916–1917, p. 324), summarized the situation:

> The Jews of America, who had greatly increased in number in the preceding twenty years, a large proportion of the increase having come from Russia, were deeply stirred by these outrages against their down-trodden and persecuted brethren. The feeling was universal among them that united action was imperatively needed. ... First, to take steps to the end that these barbarities might cease and never recur; second, that material aid be promptly extended.

The group of Jews best fitted by their influence and affluence to fulfill these objectives were the leaders of the "establishment"—Jacob Schiff, Oscar Straus, Mayer Sulzberger, Louis Marshall, Cyrus Adler, the Lewisohns, the Guggenheims et al. As the chief architect of the proposed body, Louis Marshall wrote to the president of B'nai B'rith, Adolf Kraus:

THE AMERICAN JEWISH COMMITTEE

356 SECOND AVENUE

NEW YORK

March 20, 1914.

Dear Sir:

  We beg to call your attention to the accompanying Seventh Annual Report of the American Jewish Committee, covering the work of the Committee for the year 1913.

  During that year, the Committee, which was organized to prevent the infraction of the civil and religious rights of Jews, and to alleviate the consequences of persecution, has occupied itself with a number of problems of Jewish interest. It has raised funds for the relief of the Jewish sufferers during the Balkan War; it interested our State Department in securing for those Jews who were formerly Turkish subjects and now subjects of the Balkan Allies, guarantees of civil, political and religious equality; it has interested itself in the problems of the Jews of Roumania and Russia; it has opposed the restriction of immigration to this country by a literacy test, which would have barred thousands of Jews who are emigrating from Russia and Roumania because of the impossible conditions under which they live in those countries; and it has been active in a number of other ways.

  We are sending you this report in the hope that you may find in it matters which may be of interest to the members of your organization.

    Very truly yours,

    Herman Bernstein

      Secretary.

> We all recognize that there is in the air a general desire for the
> formation of some central organization. . . . It has . . . occurred
> to some of us, that a number of leading Jews, say twenty or
> twenty-five . . . should be invited to quietly confer . . . whether
> or not it is desirable to form such a central body.

Those who were called together, men "who have for some
time past dealt with the serious problems which confront the
Jewish people," formed the American Jewish Committee. It was
to be a body of the elite, limited to sixty American citizens
directed by a tightly knit executive committee. That its purview
extended beyond concern for pogrom victims is evident from
the concept of Judge Sulzberger, which Marshall conveyed with
approval to Cyrus Adler in 1905:

> He would favor a prominent Russo-Jewish relief organization,
> with the idea that the union . . . having once been formed and
> brought into working order, would evolve automatically on a
> safe and practical basis to act in subjects other than of relieving
> the Russian situation.

A history of the committee published in its Ninth Annual
Report (1916) puts it plainly:

> The Russian massacres merely served to crystalize the feeling
> that an organization of the Jews in this country . . . was essential
> to the proper and beneficial development of the Jewish people in
> the United States.

The plight of Jews abroad afforded the committee's founders
the opportunity to institutionalize their leadership. The eastern
European immigrant Jew would accept such hegemony, for his
European experience prepared him for a leadership whose chief
virtue was acceptance by governmental authorities. He would
perceive these American *shtadlanim* as organizing to aid his
sore beset brethren in the old country; the American government would find this leadership acceptable and congenial, for it

was comprised of prominent leaders of American finance, business, and law; the American public would hail public-spirited men joining together in formal fashion to lend succor to victims of oppression. In sum, to posit the founding of the committee as a response to the challenge of providing for the needs of persecuted brethren abroad made the committee acceptable to all elements. Once established, it expanded its efforts to rights at home, and in the 1920s to a defense of the Jewish position in America in the face of a growing anti-Semitism. Its continuing posture as the champion of Jewish rights abroad gained it a certain legitimacy as being the "official" spokesman for American Jewry, which greater involvement in the internal life of the American Jew would have vitiated.

At the height of its power and influence it was the "central address" of American Jewry in matters affecting the total community. It exerted power because of its elite composition and because it was deemed to speak for the "total community." It remained an elite establishment because it was also able to confer power on those chosen to lead it. Paradoxically, although it was comprised of that element of American Jewry farthest removed from the immigrant community, its greatest usefulness was precisely to that community in its struggle to attain acceptance and status in the American social order. Its significant accomplishments in the fight against anti-Semitism in the 1920s, against racism in the 1930s, and against bigotry in the 1940s and 1950s were in large measure due to the quality of lay and professional leadership it was able to attract because of its elitist posture.

5.

Democracy from Above:
Congress and Conference

The American Jewish Committee was elitist in composition, oligarchic in organization, "prudent" in operation, and non-Zionist in ideology—all of which were opposed by elements and interests in the emerging Jewish community. Eastern European Jews were aspiring to leadership as democratic tendencies made their appearance in Jewish communal enterprise. More dynamic and forceful endeavors in behalf of Jewish well-being at home and abroad were being advocated, and a growing Zionist movement was winning adherents in the German as well as the Russian Jewish communities.

One of the reasons for the vigor of Louis Marshall's advocacy of a committee of those who had for "some time past dealt with serious problems" was to forestall the formation of a more democratically constituted body by the bright young star on the Jewish communal horizon, Dr. Judah Magnes. Marshall's persuasion succeeded in thwarting Magnes's plan. But the sentiments for a democratically constituted, more Zionistic, more militant central Jewish body persisted. Once again, a crisis situation in the life of brethren abroad gave the impetus. The outbreak of World War I prompted a Zionist conference in New York formally to propose the convening of an American Jewish

Congress. In 1915 an organization committee was constituted. It proposed the formation of a single body, popularly elected, to represent the total American Jewish community in all problems confronting it, but especially to concern itself with the political and civil rights of Jews abroad. The proposal was opposed by the American Jewish Committee, but on reconsideration it agreed to participate in a congress which would be temporary, which would be limited in function, and which would not meet until the war was over.

By 1915 the Jewish community of the United States had grown to two and a half million. Eastern European Jews outnumbered those from the west by some ten to one. They would proceed with their plans, even if the committee persisted in its opposition. To remain aloof would expose the committee to accusations of having a most limited constituency, of antidemocratic tendencies. Acting in its accustomed prudent manner, it opted to participate, wresting the conditions: that the congress limit its agenda to Jewish rights abroad; that it refrain from ideological pronouncements; that the autonomy of all existing Jewish organizations remain inviolate; that its mandate extend only to one year past the signing of the peace treaty; and that in addition to the democratically elected delegates there also be representatives of the national Jewish organizations.

Elections, in which some three hundred fifty thousand ballots were cast, were duly held. The national organizations appointed their representatives, and the congress was convened in Philadelphia on December 15, 1918. Its main order of business was the election of a delegation to represent American Jewry at the peace conference with a view toward securing for their European brethren legally recognized rights in the "new or enlarged states of Europe." It was to ask of the peace conference recognition of the aspirations and historic claims of the Jewish people in regard to Palestine, and recognition of the Balfour Declaration's promise to aid in the development of Palestine into a Jewish commonwealth.

The delegation chosen consisted of men representative of all elements of the Jewish community: German Jews and Russian Jews, Zionists and non-Zionists, Traditionalists, Reform Jews, and leaders of the labor class. Its work done, the delegation returned to New York, was tendered a reception and banquet, and prepared for the report session. On May 30, 1920, in Philadelphia, Louis Marshall presented the report on its efforts, and as per agreement, the congress was adjourned *sine die.*

A number of delegates, mainly from the Zionist and Orthodox groups and from *landsmanshaften,* reassembled the next day, and under the leadership of Stephen S. Wise called for a reconstituted congress as a permanent organization.

The stated purpose of this new national body was little different from that of the American Jewish Committee: "to further and promote Jewish rights . . . generally to deal with all matters relating to and affecting specific Jewish interests." It was no more democratically constituted than the committee, although its leadership was more representative of the wider gamut of Jewish communal interests and sentiments. In ideology it was Zionist, in structure more formally representative than the committee, and in manner more militant. Like the committee its interests and activities became more and more directed toward domestic concerns and problems, and like the committee it became a national Jewish organization with a limited agenda of interests, rather than a national representative body of the total Jewish community. In the 1930s it did effectively alert the Jewish and the American community to the growing danger of Nazism, and in the 1940s and 1950s it was in the vanguard of the forces laboring to expand democracy and extend freedom.

Committee and congress became expressions of the diversity which obtained in the Jewish community, rather than of the unity. The unity which existed was a unity of shared sentiments, concerns, apprehensions, and aspirations, particularly when they touched on the plight of Jews overseas. It was a unity which could not be contained in organizational forms in the pluralistic community which was American Jewry. Thus there was unity when the American Jew needed to take that posture in service of brethren in need; but within the family, the diversity which waves of immigration produced continued to add volatility and vitality to American Jewish communal life.

Another World War and its impending peace conference gave birth to the most ambitious attempt at American Jewish unity. The urgency was created by reports on the Holocaust. The Zionist bodies had prepared the ground. Henry Monsky, first eastern European president of B'nai B'rith, caught the vision. In its service he placed his considerable skills in organization and diplomacy. With the stipulation that the convened body be called conference and not assembly, and that it be disbanded on the accomplishment of its mission, the American Jewish Committee and the Jewish Labor Committee joined, assuring the participation of all major Jewish organizations.

One remembers the great activity and expectancy that surrounded this communal enterprise in 1943. The elections held in the local Jewish communities could open old communal wounds and create new ones, but they also placed on the communal agenda the great problems confronting American and world Jewry. The sacredness of the cause and the scope of the endeavor healed the wounds, and the communities rose recuperated and rejuvenated, reaching new levels of maturity and responsibility. The sense of being part of a united national federation elevated the local communities above parochial concerns. Heretofore disparate groups and interests were joined together in commitment to the welfare of fellow Jews in desperate plight.

One also remembers the thrill of seeing the leadership of American Jewry taking counsel together, of rising as one in denunciation of the *protestrabbiner* and their followers who greeted the conference with the establishment of the anti-Zionist American Council for Judaism, of resoundingly pledging the combined might of a united community in service of a nation to be reborn in the ancient homeland.

There were those who dared hope that this mighty organiza-

OFFICIAL COMMUNICATION

TO BE READ AT THE NEXT MEETING OF YOUR ORGANIZATION.

Chicago, February 1st, 1916

Officers and Members:—

The members of your organization are invited and urged to familiarize themselves with the inclosed resolutions, and in the interest of the movement, they should be read and re-read at your meetings. It is not an overstatement to say that the present movement for a National Jewish Congress is the most important which has engaged the attention of the Jewish people in two thousand years. It is nothing less than to bring about an end to all legal and official discrimination against the Jews everywhere.

The Executive Committee of the Jewish Congress Association assume that by participating in this Convention of representatives of more than 100,000 Jews of the Middle West, your organization realizes the importance of this movement. The fact that the movement is democratic and representative is also important, for the purpose of the movement is thereby given the moral and political strength of millions behind it.

Being democratic in its organization, it is also essential that this movement be financially democratic and independent; in other words, it should be self-supporting, and not dependent upon the largess of any powerful individual or group. To properly achieve the ends of the organization, therefore, and also to maintain its democratic spirit and structure, it is essential that its financial requirements be met by the rank and file, and that the financial burdens and sacrifices which may become necessary shall be distributed as evenly as possible among the many thousands who are now enrolled in its ranks. You are therefore called upon to contribute your proportion of the initial per capita tax of 10 cents, authorized by the Convention and levied by the Executive Committee, which will amount to $ 5.90. If we are misinformed as to the membership of your organization, as shown by this communication, kindly advise our secretary in writing.

The resolution of the Convention calls for a payment of that tax within thirty days. This amount, therefore, should be remitted not later than February 22nd, 1916. If your organization cannot collect this per capita tax in time to remit it by that date, we suggest that a proper proceeding would be that the amount be advanced out of the treasury and refunded by the usual processes later on.

Trusting in your loyalty to this great movement, and to your interest in the fate of the great Jewish People, of whom you are a part, we are.

Sincerely yours,

THE EXECUTIVE COMMITTEE OF THE JEWISH
CONGRESS ASSOCIATION FOR THE MIDDLE WEST.

JACOB G. GROSSBERG, President.   LEO H. HOFFMAN, Secretary

EDWIN T. ROMBERG, Chairman of Committee on Finance.

tion welded together by the needs of European Jewry might also address itself to the problems confronting the postwar American Jew. But the Jewish community was not ready for a permanent representative body which would impinge upon the power and programs of the existing national organizations. The American Jewish Committee, outvoted in conference, withdrew. Others resigned in protest against the withdrawal. After a half dozen years of life, the conference receded into American Jewish history. But its mere convening served its purpose, for it gave dramatic demonstration that American Jewry *was* united in concern for the plight of their brethren in wartorn Europe, and resolutions adopted declared that the united community saw a Jewish commonwealth in Palestine as the chief means for the amelioration of their plight.

The reasons the attempts at establishing a representative body of American Jewry failed are many: the diversity of a community, made more diverse by continuing immigration; the pluralistic climate of America; the voluntary nature of the American Jewish community; and the example from the American political scene of "nonpartisan" politics in external affairs, but never in domestic matters. The hopes raised by the unity engendered by response to crises overseas may well have blinded the leadership to the substantial problems standing in the way of an organizationally united American Jewry.

To these one must add another. Such unity as was attempted was a unity imposed from above, from a national body welded by the crisis of the moment. True unity can come only from the grassroots desire of individuals to join in communities, and of those communities to federate into a national body. Such a unity, we believe, is beginning to take shape in the American Jewish community. But the roots of such unity, the influences which shaped it, and the road it has traversed are different, as we shall see.

II

TO
AID
A
BROTHER

There is no brighter chapter in the whole history of philanthropy than that which could be written of the work of the American Jews.

—Herbert Hoover, 1923

6.

"That They May Not Hunger and Perish"

Aid to brethren overseas began early in American Jewish experience. The first Palestinian emissary to collect funds for the Jews in the Holy Land, Moses Malki, arrived in 1759. There were barely a thousand Jews in the American colonies at the time, but the funds collected were sufficient to encourage another to come to these shores a dozen years later. "The venerable Hocham, the Learned Rabbi, Haijm Isaac Karigal, of the City of Hebron, near Jerusalem in the Holy Land," arrived in Philadelphia in the summer of 1772. After a month there, he spent half a year in New York, and then moved to Newport, Rhode Island, where he made a profound impression on the entire community. His Shavuot sermon was published in that seaport city in 1773, and his portrait hangs at Yale.

Palestinian emissaries came to the United States throughout the nineteenth century and continue to the present day. Aaron Selig brought news of the Holy Land and collected funds for its needy Jews in 1849–1850, in New York, Baltimore, Cincinnati, Louisville, New Orleans, Mobile, Montgomery, Charleston, Richmond, New Haven, Boston, Albany, Utica, Syracuse, and Rochester. A little more than a quarter of a century later Nathan Neta Netkin reached the West Coast and was able to report collections of $101.00 in Los Angeles, $75.00 in Sacramento, $85.00 in Maryville, $18.50 in Grass Valley, $45.00 in Stockton, and over $250 in San Francisco.

Most of the collecting was done through congregations or special committees set up for that purpose. Throughout the century private individuals sent contributions as well. Thus Moses Heyman of Sacramento received a letter of acknowledgment from Sir Moses Montefiore in 1860: "In compliance with your request I forwarded your remittance of £6 ($31.00) for the benefit of the poor in Jerusalem to the Representatives of the different congregations in the Holy City and requested them to acknowledge receipt thereof at their earliest convenience."

So zealous was Moses Hyman of Cincinnati for the cause that in 1867 he sold all his belongings and set out for the Holy Land, collecting funds on the way to aid in building housing in Jerusalem for the Jewish settlers. His mission accomplished, he returned and spent the rest of his days as the most ardent supporter of Palestine relief in his city. An anonymous pamphlet, published in Jerusalem in 1868, describes and extols the visit of "Mr. Moses Hyman and his son, Solomon, of Cincinnati" to the school Doresh Zion.

Two years earlier a poem by Jacob Saphir, scribe of the community of Jerusalem, welcomed the arrival of Sir Moses Montefiore to Jerusalem, bringing with him the $60,000 that Judah Touro of New Orleans had left in his will for the poor of the Holy Land. Mishkenot Shaananim, the first housing built outside the city walls, is the monument to this most generous of benefactors.

As early as 1833, a society called Terumat Ha-Kodesh was organized in New York to collect funds for Palestine without recourse to emissaries, and continued its work for many years. Twenty years later the American Relief Society for Indigent Jews in Jerusalem, Palestine, was founded; it soon received a legacy of $10,000 from the estate of Judah Touro, and thereafter remitted an income of $700.00 annually. Isaac Leeser, in his

New York, May 8th, 1903.

Dear Sir :—

Great distress prevails at Kischineff, Russia, by reason of the Anti-Semitic riots last week, wherein we are informed that more than one hundred persons of the Jewish faith were killed, from five to six hundred were injured, and many others were made homeless and suffered the destruction of their property. The *Alliance Israélite Universelle* has cabled requesting our co-operation in securing financial relief, stating that several million francs are needed for this purpose. After a discussion of the situation, we believe that this community should co-operate liberally with the *Alliance Israélite* in providing relief; and your subscription is therefore solicited. In view of the necessities of the case, you are urged to send promptly whatever contribution you may desire to make, to MR. DANIEL GUGGENHEIM, Treasurer of the Relief Fund, 71 Broadway, New York City.

Yours truly,

EMANUEL LEHMAN, CHAIRMAN,	LOUIS MARSHALL,
NATHAN BIJUR,	HENRY RICE,
JOSEPH B. BLOOMINGDALE,	JACOB H. SCHIFF,
SIMON BORG,	ISAAC N. SELIGMAN,
DANIEL GUGGENHEIM,	LOUIS STERN,
CHARLES L. HALLGARTEN,	ISIDOR STRAUS,
MYER S. ISAACS,	CYRUS L. SULZBERGER,
MORRIS LOEB,	ISAAC WALLACH.

41

Occident, urged aid, and Samuel Isaac's *Jewish Messenger* was particularly devoted to the cause.

From time to time campaigns were organized to aid Jews in particular plight, like the one launched by the Board of Delegates of American Israelites in 1859, in behalf of "the Jews of Tangiers, in Morocco, who, to the number of upwards of three thousand, have been landed at Gibraltar . . . to escape from the barbarous and lawless Kabyles. . . . The aged and infirm, the young and robust, the mother and her offspring, appeal for succor, that they may not HUNGER and PERISH."

The campaign was carried on through the congregations, as were most charitable efforts for overseas needs during the nineteenth century. Causes such as the plight of Roumanian Jewry in the 1870s and Russian Jews in the 1880s elicited not only protest but charitable endeavors as well.

The mass immigration from eastern Europe, which doubled the size of the Jewish community in America in each of the three decades from 1880 to 1910, strained the charitable capacity of American Jewry to the limit. Immigrant reception and settlement, settlement houses, orphanages, schools, and a network of social service agencies not only laid claim on American philanthropic monies, but also sought and received aid from abroad. Nevertheless, the Alliance Israelite solicited and gathered contributions for its own institutions in the countries of the Levant, and both private and public monies went to eastern European communities ravaged and reduced to poverty.

Overseas aid in the twentieth century grew with the community. The pogroms in Russia in 1903 and 1905 were met with demonstrations, with political activity, and above all, with philanthropic generosity.

A contemporary report of events in 1903 by Rabbi Maximillian Heller attests:

Realizing that America was the chief refuge of all victims of persecution, the people of the United States became the world's logical leaders in a campaign of humanity. . . . Great meetings of

protest were held all over the country. . . . Large sums of money
were collected by journals, churches, committees. . . .

Like every other great sorrow Kishineff has brought the Jews
of the world nearer to one another. . . . It gave American Jewry
the hegemony of the world's Judaism by proving that American
Jews have the courage and the public spirit openly to espouse the
cause of their brothers.

But all the efforts, zealous and generous as they may have
been, were the undertakings of groups of special interest and
motivation. It was not till World War I that a united,
community-wide ongoing effort which involved all segments of
American Jewry was launched. The great campaigns during the
war years and the years which followed brought relief to the
impoverished and ravished community of the Old World, and a
sense of unity and common destiny to the Jews of the New.

7.

"Appeal to Their Brethren in America"

In September of 1914, twenty-eight-year-old Maurice Wertheim debarked in Palestine's port city, Jaffa, from the cruiser U.S.S. *North Carolina*, carrying a suitcase filled with "the equivalent of fifty thousand dollars." He had brought the money from Constantinople at the request of his father-in-law, the Hon. Henry Morgenthau, United States ambassador to Turkey. In a letter to "Messrs. Jacob H. Schiff, Louis Marshall, Nathan Straus, and Members of the American Jewish Committee, New York City," dated October 21, 1914, he reported:

> the relief sent so promptly by American Jews and on an American warship produced a tremendous impression throughout all Palestine, and has, I think, done a great deal for the prestige of the Jews of Palestine.

Louis Marshall, president, pointed out to the members of the committee at the eighth annual meeting, "Among the earliest victims of the war were the Jews of Palestine." He reminded his colleagues that most of the Jewish residents of the Holy Land were dependent on the "benevolence of their co-religionists in Europe and America." With the outbreak of the war, aid from

Europe had come to an end. All depended now on the Jews of America.

Toward the end of August of that fateful year, Ambassador Morgenthau had sent "urgent cablegrams" to the American Jewish Committee alerting it to the desperate plight of Palestinian Jewry and requesting an immediate grant of fifty thousand dollars. The committee responded at once. As was his wont, Jacob H. Schiff took leadership, pledging a quarter of the requested amount. The committee itself appropriated $25,000 from its Emergency Trust Fund. It invited the Federation of American Zionists to "complete the sum required." Mr. Marshall reported, "That organization promptly responded, turning over the required sum to the Committee."

Wertheim, who supervised the distribution of the funds he brought, reported to the committee on the "actual conditions" he found, and sent the "Plan of Distribution" worked out on the committee's cabled instructions that "while the money should be placed wherever it would afford the greatest relief, preference should be given to its use in a productive manner that would bear results beyond the mere distribution of bread and money." The country was divided into three districts and nine subdivisions, supervised by a general committee and administered by local committees who were empowered to allocate the monies "in the manner they deem best." These principles were designed to make the monies spent ameliorative and not merely palliative. The good offices of the American consul were engaged and arrangements were made to "secure protection . . . from the Turkish authorities." Dr. Arthur Ruppin was to be chairman of the general committee and would render monthly reports to Louis Marshall.

This "plan" provided the first "rational" distribution of funds gathered abroad in support of the Jews of the Holy Land. Heretofore, attempts at just and equitable distribution of funds foundered in the shoals of "ethnic" division and animosities between the Sephardi and Ashkenazi communities, and within the latter between the various *landsmanshaft kolelim*. Now a more just, reasonable, and productive distribution was to be made by local committees, "*but only* in accordance with the general principles" laid down by the contributor agency. A partnership was thus effected between American Jewry and the Yishuv for an ad hoc enterprise, but it laid the foundation for cooperation between world Jewry and the Yishuv in the organized joint planning for the development of the Jewish community in Palestine.

This pioneer effort had its long-range effect on American Jewry as well. It joined in common enterprise the non-Zionist and Zionist elements, and set the stage for the disparate components of the American Jewish community—German Jews and eastern European Jews, Orthodox and Reform, socialists and capitalists—to work together. It was a significant first step in the long and rocky road toward Jewish unity in America. In 1914 the plight of brethren abroad erased ideological and organizational differences at home.

Marshall pointed out that "the amounts thus far forwarded will afford only temporary relief" for the Jews of Palestine. He foresaw that "as soon as they can communicate . . . the Jews of Russia, Belgium, Austria-Hungary . . . will appeal to their brethren in America."

The first to hear this appeal was the Orthodox Jewish community. On September 28, 1914, the Rev. Dr. Bernard Drachman, president of the Union of Orthodox Jewish Congregations, sent telegrams to eighty congregations, urging: "Our unfortunate brethren abroad are suffering the terrors of a frightful war. Your congregation is requested to make offerings on Kol Nidre Eve."

A month later the union, the Mizrachi, the Agudas Harabonim, and the Central Committee of Palestine Institutions joined to form the Central Committee for the Relief of the Jews Suffering Through the War.

It is not surprising that the Orthodox community was the first in organizing for relief. It had both the most immediate motivation and a ready vehicle for solicitation and collection.

To the recently arrived immigrants from what was now the war zone of eastern Europe, the suffering there was not only of fellow Jews but of members of their families. The "First Official War Relief Appeal Addressed to American Jewry October 14, by the Central Relief Committee" stressed:

> Remember—No one can tell, today, whether his own relatives are not refugees far from their own home.
> Remember—You cannot know where your own father or mother, sister or brother is. Your help, through us, may help them.

A network of synagogues in which charitable contributions were a daily occurrence, and rabbis who engaged in constant solicitation for all manner of worthy causes, provided the sites and manpower for the raising of "an enormous amount of money at once . . . and to continue the effort . . . possibly even through the next few years to come!"

It soon became apparent to all that raising the "enormous amount of money" which the situation demanded would need an unprecedented effort of a united community, under the leadership of Schiff, Marshall, Warburg et al. To launch such an effort, a conference was convened by the American Jewish Committee on October 25, 1914. The national organizations represented reached across the entire gamut of the American Jewish community. The Orthodox Agudas Harabonim and Union of Orthodox Jewish Congregations joined with the Reform Central Conference of American Rabbis and Union of American Hebrew Congregations and the Conservative United Synagogues of America; the Federation of American Zionists sat with the anti-Zionist Arbeiter Ring; Jewish fraternal orders came to express fraternal concern.

A crisis abroad, the plight of fellow Jews, and the enterprise of coming to their aid "to accomplish the largest measure of relief" brought unity to an American Jewry divided by ethnic, religious, economic, and social differences. Radical Reformer and pious Orthodox, Jewish nationalist and zealous socialist, German Jew and Russian Jew were joined in a community of concern and compassion.

The conference appointed a committee of five—Oscar Straus, the first Jew to serve in the cabinet; the Hon. Julian W. Mack and Louis D. Brandeis, American-born "establishment Jews" become Zionists; Orthodox leader Harry Fischel; and Meyer London, labor lawyer and the first Socialist to serve in Congress—a body representative of and respected by all elements of the community, and charged them to select one hundred leading American Jews to constitute the American Jewish Relief Committee. Louis Marshall was to be president and Felix M. Warburg, treasurer.

The committee set to work at once, organizing a campaign to extend through the entire community. It soon became obvious that although overseas needs made for unity, realities at home made for the retention of diversity. Different groups had different forms of appeal, different modes of operation; their constituents lived in different areas and spoke different languages. So long as these differences obtained it would be easier and more effective to accept them and permit the campaign to mirror the diversity in the community.

The Central Relief Committee remained the campaign apparatus of the Orthodox community, and the American Jewish Relief Committee that of the German Jewish establishment. On November 27, 1914, they organized the Joint Distribution Committee of American Funds for the Relief of Jewish War Sufferers, and chose Felix M. Warburg to be its chairman. A few months later the eastern European socialist labor element formed the People's Relief Committee under the chairmanship of the Hon. Meyer London and joined the other two.

Each committee carried on its campaign in its own manner. The American Jewish Relief Committee set the tone. Its mass meetings inaugurated the campaigns. The large gifts announced set the standards for giving. In 1915 only $1.5 million was raised for the Joint Distribution Committee. In 1916 Nathan

Straus pledged $100,000 and urged a target of $5 million. President Wilson declared a Jewish War Sufferers Relief Day, the Red Cross aided in the collection, and before the year was out the goal urged by Straus was nearly met. The following year, Dr. Judah Magnes returned from the war zone demanding that a goal of $10 million be set. At a great rally in Carnegie Hall which he addressed, the quota became realizable when Julius Rosenwald made the first of his great pledges, $1 million, conditional on the goal's being met. It was.

The Central Relief Committee sold War Relief Stamps and War Relief Certificates, conducted appeals in synagogues, and sponsored cantorial concerts and a tour by the most renowned cantorial artist, Yosele Rosenblatt, which opened in New York's Hippodrome and brought in $70,000. A Tag Day, collections in the Garment District, pledges of days of labor, and newspaper solicitations raised funds for the People's Relief Committee.

Each committee had a style appropriate to its clientele. But all joined in entrusting their funds to the Joint Distribution Committee, which during the war years distributed some $20 million. A 1916 report stated: "All the funds collected by the three relief committees are administered by the Joint Distribution Committee working through various organizations and individuals in the countries at war or affected by the war."

In Russia the funds were entrusted to the Jewish Committee for Relief of Sufferers from the War in Petrograd. In German-occupied Poland, Das Judisches Hilfskomite für Polen administered the aid, and the Israelitische Allianz aus Wien did the same for the Jews in Austria-Hungary and in territories occupied by its armies. The American embassy at Constantinople conveyed JDC funds "for distribution through committees accredited to it." In Palestine, Dr. Otis A. Glazenbrook, United States consul at Jerusalem, aided the committee in its work.

The division which obtained in the American Jewish community necessitated "three relief committees," but the unified distribution of funds caused European Jewry to perceive American

The First Official War Relief Appeal

Addressed to American Jewry, October, 1914,
by the Central Relief Committee

To the Jews of America:

Our brethren are dying. Widows and orphans are wandering, homeless, naked and hungry. Women, old and young, with their little ones, and the aged find no refuge. In every land that we or our fathers once called home, bloody war with all its unspeakable horrors stalks abroad; thousands of villages have been ravaged and great cities laid waste. Mourning, they lift up their eyes, whence shall come their help!

More than half of the Jews of the world are overwhelmed in the present conflict. The condition of our brethren in Palestine, also, is past description. Its institutions can no longer be supported by the generosity of our brethren in Europe, as to-day the Jews of Europe are themselves sore beset.

Another most serious condition brought about by the war must not be overlooked. Thousands among us have regularly sent money to our families and friends "at home" to help our less fortunate kinsmen.

All the world is looking to us for aid and direction. We will surely not be deaf to their prayers.

We have therefore formed in New York a committee of representative rabbis and laymen to help our co-religionists in Europe and Palestine.

This committee is extending its organization throughout the United States and appeals to you to join it. It asks you either to call a meeting in your synagogue, or to join with others to call a meeting in your city, at which contributions shall be collected, local officers elected and representatives chosen to be added to our Central Committee in New York. We want at least two representatives in each city of the United States to be in constant communication with us, in order to organize the Jews of America into one compact body, ready and willing to raise a large

RELIEF FUND FOR JEWS SUFFERING THROUGH THE WAR

REMEMBER—This war has ruined hundreds of thousands of our brethren.

REMEMBER—No one can tell, today, whether his own relatives are not refugees far from their own home.

REMEMBER—That the assistance of this Committee may save the lives of those who are near and dear to you. You cannot know where your own father or mother, sister or brother is. Your help through us, may help them.

AND REMEMBER—That this war will cause an amount of suffering unprecedented in history. Ways and means must be devised to raise an enormous amount of money at once, and to continue the effort throughout the weeks and months, aye, possibly even through the next few years to come!

This Committee is preparing plans which will enable every one to help daily, weekly and monthly, without taxing the resources of any one beyond his means.

Join us at once. Send in your name and the names of those associated with you to the secretary of the committee. The Union of Orthodox Jewish Congregations of America, The Agudas Harabonim, The Mizrachi and the Central Committee of Palestine Institutions are all represented on this committee. A large number of collections have already been made in response to their appeals. All amounts should be remitted as soon as possible to the financial secretary of this committee; and checks drawn made payable to the order of the treasurer.

Five thousand dollars has been sent to a committee of Palestinian Jews, comprising Guedalia N. Broder, Isaac Chagis, Joseph Eliaschar, Behr Epstein, Saul Isaac Freund, Dr. Isaac Levy, Solomon Perlman, Alter Rivlin, Dr. Arthur Ruppin, Solomon Rubin, Wolf Schocher, Salmon Soloweitchik, Aaron Vallero, David Yellin.

Five thousand dollars has been sent to the Israelitische Alliance, Vienna, for the relief of Galician Jews and one thousand dollars for the Yeshibath.

In securing the services of Mr. Harry Fischel as Treasurer, the Committee has obtained the advantage of his wide acquaintance throughout the United States. All moneys received by him are deposited in The Guaranty Trust Company of America. Arrangements will be made through the accredited representatives of the U. S. Government to forward money to our stricken brethren, as soon as we can get in touch with responsible people in all the war zones, who will distribute it without favor for the immediate relief of the Jewish widows and orphans, sick and wounded, aged and infirm, in short, to all those who will die of hunger and cold, unless you promptly help.

Leon Kamaiky, Chairman
Harry Fischel, Treasurer,
World Bldg., 63 Park Row, New York

J. A. Bernstein, Recording Secretary
Morris Engelman, Financial Secretary
Albert Lucas, Corresponding Secretary

November 17.—Twenty cases of clothing sent to Belgian Jewish refugees in England, collected by Albert Lucas.

November 22.—Meeting at Hotel Astor, New York City, of the Committee of 100 organized as the American Jewish Relief Committee to elect an Executive Committee of 25.

November 27.—American Jewish Relief Committee and the Central Relief Committee organized the Joint Distribution Committee, electing Mr. Felix M. Warburg, Chairman.

December 20.—Mr. Felix M. Warburg, Chairman of the Joint Distribution Committee, presided at a meeting of the Landsmanschaften, called for the purpose of obtaining their cooperation for War Relief.

December 31.—Mr. M. Engelman toured the Middle Western States to introduce War Relief Stamps.

1915

January 1.—Mr. Felix M. Warburg, Chairman, Joint Distribution Committee, organized a Remittance Bureau, supervised by Miss Harriet B. Lowenstein.
Up to August 1, 1918, handled 24,658 remittances amounting to $607,808.32.

January 12.—Twenty-four cases of clothing forwarded to Austria, through the efforts of Mr. Albert Lucas.

March 10.—U. S. Collier Vulcan sailed for Palestine with a cargo of foodstuffs consigned to Palestine.

May 1.—Certificates ranging in value from $1.00 to $5.00 bearing the fac-simile signatures of the officers of the American Jewish Relief Committee and the Central Committee, were introduced by Mr. Engelman.

National Officers

—

Louis Marshall
President

Cyrus L. Sulzberger
Secretary

Felix M. Warburg
Treasurer

—

Troy Officers

—

H. H. BUTLER
Chairman

W. FRIEDMAN
Vice-Chairman

H. KUSCHEWSKY
Secretary

CHARLES LAUB
Treasurer

HEADQUARTERS

Troy Jewish Relief Committee

For the Relief of Jewish War Sufferers

166 RIVER STREET

TROY, N. Y.

January
22nd,
1916.

My Dear Sir:-

     President Wilson, in compliance with a resolution of the Senate, designated January 27th

     "as a day upon which the people of the United States may make such contributions as they feel disposed for the aid of the stricken Jewish people."

     Of the Nine Million Jews in the war zones of Europe a majority of them are destitute of food, shelter and clothing. They have been driven from their homes without any warning and suffer from starvation and disease.

     The Troy Jewish Relief Committee was appointed the official representative of the American Jewish Relief Committee to receive contributions to the $5,000,000 fund being raised by the Jews of the United States.

     Thus far we have met with very encouraging success from all, regardless of race or creed, and we assure you that the Jews of Troy feel deeply appreciative for the generous assistance offered them by their neighbors.

     We trust that you will feel inclined to answer this call of humanity and extend a helping hand to relieve the suffering of our brethren in the war stricken countries.

     Contributions may be mailed to Mr. Charles Laub, Treasurer, 46 Third Street, Troy, N. Y.

              H. H. BUTLER, Chairman,

Mayor CORNELIUS F. BURNS,
Rev. Dr. H. R. FREEMAN,
Rev. Dr. H. R. LASKER,
Rev. Dr. D. KLEINFELD,
Rt. Rev. JOHN WALSH,
Mr. HENRY GROSS,
Mr. THOMAS VAIL,

Mr. WM. LELAND THOMPSON,
Mr. H. G. HAMMETT,
Mr. JOSEPH A. LEGGETT,
Mr. JACOB ELLIS,
Mr. JAMES GOLDSTONE,
Mr. B. KRAUS,
Mr. JOSEPH T. FOXELL.

Promptness Spells Success — Delay Spells Suffering

SUMMARY

1. The relief problem of the Jews in Poland constitute the greatest Jewish relief problem in the world.

2. Overseas Unit No. 1 has achieved success in its endeavors to cope with the situation in Poland.

(a) Through its branch offices it transacts the many relief and rehabilitation activities.

(b) Through its central administration it conducts important functional activities.

(c) Perhaps its greatest value lies in the effect of the presence of uniformed American Jewish relief workers to raise the courage and to adjust relationships between them, and other non-sectarian departments.

3. Poland, from the relief standpoint, cannot be considered as a whole—it divides itself into four areas which might be designated as Congress Poland, the Bialystok-Brest-Litowsk-Wilno-Minsk territory, Galicia and Rowno territory. Conditions and problems differ in each of these areas. Congress Poland is more or less removed from war operations, Galicia still suffers especially in its smaller communities, from its direct result. Rowno territory and the Bialystok-Brest-Litowsk-Wilno-Minsk territory are experiencing actual war at this time.

4. Various special functional activities are being developed by the JDC in Poland and require special attention.

(a) About sixty thousand orphans are uncared for; a beginning at meeting this problem has been made by placing children in private homes and in institutions, and allowing a per capita subvention for their care, thus retaining supervision and control over the care of each child thus cared for.

3

(b)   The medical activities are greatly handicapped by lack of adequate trained personnel, both doctors and nurses.   Plans are projected for the establishment of nurses' training centers.

(c)   Activities for constructive relief are being inaugurated gradually because of the certainty of political and economic developments.   However, sufficient activities are being initiated to form the basis for future activities and to offer a basis of real experience upon which to build.   The types of constructive work available are loans to co-operatives, artisans and small dealers, establishment of trade schools, distribution of tools and building of houses.

(d)   The designation by local committees of part of the relief funds for cultural activities leads to critical problems in the relief work.   Funds actually needed for the alleviation of appalling material needs are diverted for cultural purposes and become the bone of contention between struggling political factions.

Jewry as one united community, and made for a similar perception by the American government.

The outside observer perceives the forest; one living in it
knows the individual trees. In 1916 the perception that the
whole is greater than the sum of its parts was two generations
and many unifying enterprises away. In the war years, the
European Jewish communities began to look to the daughter
community overseas for aid and succor, and come to know it as
a concerned and generous offspring—and as a child reaching
adulthood, who would care for its parents in their need. The
American Jewish community underwent an instant maturation,
accepting the maturity and its attendant responsibilities which a
crisis evokes. It also met the challenge of the need for cooperation, for disciplining differences and for allaying animosities in
service of a cause worthy of everyone's utmost exertions and
above anyone's parochial interests. In practical terms, it learned
that even when differences and divisions continue to mark the
grassroots landscape of the community, cooperation is possible, in fact mandatory, among the designated leadership.

In the war years and those that followed, German Jews
learned to respect the ardor and selflessness of Russian Jews,
who in turn grew to appreciate the concern and generosity of
this elite group toward all Jews, everywhere. Anti-Zionists and
non-Zionists began to understand the single-minded passion of
the Zionists; they in turn learned that what divided them were
perceptions of nationalism and political loyalties and not devotion to the welfare of fellow Jews. Socialists awaiting and laboring for the social revolution turned their attention to the immediate needs of sore beset brethren, and finding their "class
antagonists" and "exploiters" engaged in similar labors, joined
hands with them.

The postwar years of 1919 and 1920 posed the challenge of a
million homeless Jews, of mass pogroms in the Ukraine, of
devastated communities attempting to reestablish themselves in
a chaotic and hostile Europe. "Bread for the Hungry—Shrouds
for the Dead" was the chilling call to American Jewry. Some

$27 million was contributed in these years, and some $20 million more by 1924. JDC workers fanned out through the wartorn landscape, organizing self-help committees, distributing food, clothing, and medicine, setting up small loan societies. The cooperation of the United States government and America's great relief agencies was sought and obtained. Generosity and skillful utilization of all available resources made the term "Joint" synonymous with saving and hope to the Jew of the ravaged continent. As Herbert Hoover observed in 1923: "There is no brighter chapter in the whole history of philanthropy than that which could be written of the work of the American Jews in the last nine years." This was not the comment of an enthusiastic campaigner, but the appraisal of a sober professional.

8.

"Enduring Cooperation on Behalf of Jewish Causes"

Joining to aid brothers in distress, American Jewry set aside rivalries. On the political scene, however, contention marked American Jewish communal life. During the first two years of the war, Zionist-oriented eastern European Jewry, now outnumbering the German Jewish element by some ten to one, challenged the leadership exerted by the American Jewish Committee. The apparent issue was the place of Palestine in the future of world Jewry, a Zionist/anti-Zionist confrontation; the stated issue was the democratization of American Jewish life; the root issue was control of and decision-making for an American Jewish community expected by all to become the leading Jewish community in the world.

The project was the creation of a democratically constituted American Jewish Congress. Louis D. Brandeis served as ideologist and strategist; Rabbi Stephen S. Wise roused the masses. At a rally of the Congress Organizing Committee on January 24, 1916, Brandeis argued that only an American Jewry united in a democratic representative body would have the power to obtain equal rights and opportunities for their brethren in Europe. Four days later Brandeis was appointed to the Supreme Court of the United States. The masses seized upon this as an omen indicating American approval of their quest for democracy in American Jewish life. Compromises proposed by the American Jewish Committee were rejected, and a conference to create a congress to meet in Philadelphia on March 27 and 28 heard Stephen S. Wise proclaim that the people

> are resolved to be free of their masters whether these be malevolent tyrants without, or benevolent despots within the life of Israel. . . . The time is come for a leadership by us to be chosen, a leadership that shall democratically and wisely lead rather than autocratically command.

To the 367 delegates from eighty-three cities representing thirty-three organizations with a combined membership of over one million, the congress would provide democracy at home and win equal rights abroad. It was a sentiment which could not be denied, and the American Jewish Committee grudgingly capitulated. It retained, however, its power of purse and influence, and for the next three decades committee and congress were joined in a struggle on all manner of issues confronting American Jews.

The committee kept its control over the relief activities during the war and in the postwar years. It provided the leadership for the major fundraising arm, the American Jewish Relief Committee, and for the Joint Distribution Committee. Zionist and democratic challenges were easily thwarted, since all major contributors, excepting only Nathan Straus, were in the non-Zionist and anti-Zionist camps which the committee represented.

The formal unity forced upon American Jewry by the crisis facing war-ravaged European Jewry began to fall apart as the situation "normalized" in the postwar world. The immediate needs of almost a million displaced persons, sixty thousand orphans, countless widows, pogrom-shattered communities, had kept the alliance intact. But discordant notes began to be heard. The Zionists claimed that not enough of the funds were being directed to Palestine, thus preventing larger numbers of Jews from settling there and fulfilling the promise held forth by the Balfour Declaration.

The fundraisers and fund providers were all opposed to political Zionism and a Jewish state. Some, like Jacob H. Schiff, Louis Marshall, and Felix Warburg, were committed to helping the Jews in Palestine as they would aid Jews anywhere; others, like the JDC's most effective fundraiser, David A. Brown, and Julius Rosenwald, the single most generous philanthropist, opposed any funds for the Yishuv. Brown felt that the JDC's responsibility was to the Jews of Europe; let the American Zionists provide for their brethren in Palestine. Rosenwald's opposition was even more pronounced, for he felt that the ancient Holy Land was no longer suitable for a modern agricultural or industrial society: "I shall not lift a finger to advance the immigration of Jews to Palestine, for Palestine has nothing to offer them. The soil is too poor to support them. Nor is Palestine a field for either manufacture or industry."

The Zionists, on the other hand, argued that the only secure future for European Jewry was in a commonwealth in Palestine. All aid to European Jewry which would encourage them to remain on that continent was a historic disservice to them. The minority rights granted them by peace treaties, they warned, were ephemeral; their hopes for equal rights, security, and well-being, chimerical.

So long as the aid provided by the "Joint" was to alleviate immediate suffering, there could be no arguing against it. But when that aid was turned to reconstructing life in what the Zionists were certain was a hostile and ultimately destructive environment, they turned forcefully against it.

The issue was joined in 1924, when the JDC established the American Jewish Joint Agricultural Corporation to handle its work in the Soviet Union, the "Agro-Joint." Within four years some $6 million had been contributed by the JDC to resettle about thirty-five thousand Jewish families on farms in the Crimea. The Zionists saw this as a direct affront and challenge.

While colonization in Palestine was languishing for want of funds, large sums were being poured into the Soviet Union.

American Jewry was still joined in fundraising for overseas needs through the United Jewish Campaign. The circular letter announcing the 1926 campaign emphasized the work in the Crimea, and made no mention of any money going for projects in Palestine. Although they had been promised $1.5 million for work in Palestine, the Zionists withdrew in anger from the United Jewish Campaign and organized a separate United Palestine Appeal in 1925. All efforts by the master conciliator, Louis Marshall, were to no avail, and the division within the community now extended to fundraising as well. It is interesting to note that of the $60 million raised by the JDC in the first decade of its existence (1916–1926), only $7 million, some 12 percent, went to Palestine.

What exacerbated the situation even further was the report of the Joint Palestine Survey Commission, consisting of Lord Melchett, Lee K. Frankel, Felix M. Warburg, and Oscar Wasserman, which warned:

> The present budget of Keren Hayesod scarcely suffices to maintain existing services. . . . It is evident that, until more funds are forthcoming, for the present no new enterprises can be undertaken. . . . The Commissioners, however, feel very strongly that a policy which does not allow of further development and the acquisition of new territory, the founding of new colonies . . . must be considered entirely unsatisfactory, and one not acceptable to the Jewish community as a whole for the carrying out of its duty and obligations.

The report urged that: "The Commissioners appeal to the entire Jewish world to make the necessary sacrifices to establish an ideal which will prove a just source of pride and satisfaction to all members of the community."

At the same time American Jewry learned that the leaders of the JDC had established an American Society for Jewish Farm Settlements in Russia, with James Rosenberg as chairman and with Louis Marshall, Herbert Lehman, and Felix Warburg as directors. A quiet drive to match a $10-million grant from the Russian government yielded some $8 million, Julius Rosenwald contributing $5 million, Felix Warburg, $1 million, and John D. Rockefeller, Jr., half a million.

From 1925, when Julian Mack, Louis D. Brandeis, and others organized the Palestine Economic Corporation with the approval and aid of the JDC, it was apparent to all that the old alliance entered into under the stress of wartime overseas needs was no longer viable. The differences in ideology and commitment were such as to make division in the fundraising enterprise advisable. American Jewry was a divided community, and it would serve no good or useful purpose to pretend that it was otherwise.

The great champion of Jewish unity in America, Louis Marshall, passed away in 1929, but not before his final and most lasting creation had been accomplished. Largely through his vision, energy, skill, and persistence, Zionists and non-Zionists joined in work for Palestine through the Jewish Agency for Palestine. That accomplished, the Joint Distribution Committee and American members of the Jewish Agency agreed to join in an Allied Jewish Campaign. Its goal was to be $6 million, of which $3 million would go to the JDC and $2.5 million to the Jewish Agency.

What gave urgency to the need for a united effort was again an overseas crisis. During 1929 bloody anti-Jewish riots in Palestine evoked unanimous sympathy and support from all segments of American Jewry (the Jewish Communists excepted). No American Jew, be he non-Zionist or anti-Zionist, could oppose aid to coreligionists victimized by pogroms and boycott.

Felix Warburg, who had been second only to Marshall in his commitment to a united American Jewry, hailed the joint campaign as the beginning of "a lasting and permanent unity in American Israel." The unity was short lived. At the campaign's end it was agreed that

the increasingly pressing need for immediate funds for the
achievements of both organizations, the differing budgetary
requirements, and the advisability of permitting as much freedom of choice and support as possible during the present trying
economic period, have made it desirable . . . to separate their
fund raising activities.

But it was also observed that "the joint drive had resulted in the
creation of important communal values and the laying of the
foundation in many communities, for enduring co-operation on
behalf of Jewish causes."

It did set a pattern for a joint campaign, attempted again in
the mid-1930s and taking permanent form in 1939 with the
creation of the United Jewish Appeal. In each instance it was the
challenge of an overseas crisis which forced united action. The
act of planning together, of campaigning with one another,
created an atmosphere of unity and reinforced the latent sentiments of Jewish oneness. The Jewish system of *Mitzvoth*
—commandments to do right—is based on the proposition
that the deed fashions the attitude. To give charity evokes
charitable sentiments. To engage in united enterprise is to
acquire a sense of unity.

9.

"A Lasting and Permanent Unity"

The Allied Jewish Campaign launched so auspiciously at a national conference held in the nation's capital on March 8, 1930, did not establish "a lasting and permanent unity in American Israel." The joint campaign itself ended on the expiration date of the agreement, December 31, 1930. During the nine months of united action, campaigns were conducted in 230 cities and towns in which $2.5 million was pledged.

The reasons for separation were couched in diplomatic language: "The increasing pressing needs for immediate funds of both organizations" meant that a joint campaign lessened the ardor of those who had very specific interests and commitments. A Zionist could not be moved to sacrificial generosity when he knew that a portion of his contribution would go to settle Jews on land in the Soviet Union; an anti-Zionist could not be persuaded to give enthusiastic support to a nationalistic enterprise in Palestine which he considered at best foolish and at worst dangerous to his own status as citizen and neighbor. "The advisability of permitting as much freedom of choice and support as possible" is the way the statement of dissolution phrased it.

The allied campaign had resulted from and was an expression

of a new sense of unity which came upon American Jewry in the latter months of 1929. In part it was due to a rapprochement of Zionists and non-Zionists marked by their joining together to form the Enlarged Jewish Agency in August 1929. Louis D. Brandeis had urged its creation; Louis Marshall was its architect. To the Zionists it promised new sources of revenue for the upbuilding of the Homeland; for the non-Zionists it offered a participation permitting influence and guidance. If the two camps could join internationally to work together in matters political, it stands to reason that they must come together for united fundraising in America. It was the American members of the Jewish Agency who signed the agreement with the JDC to join in the allied campaign.

The need to unite was given emotional motivation by the news of the Arab riots against the Jews in Palestine. In times of crisis, how dare brothers stand apart?

By the end of 1930, Louis Marshall was no longer present to lend his prestige and his skills at negotiation and conciliation. The initial shock caused by the news of pogroms in the Holy Land had worn off. Zionists could now return to their long-held feelings that the "heroic efforts" of nation building were receiving inadequate support; non-Zionists reminded themselves that their commitment was to aid in the experiment of Jewish life under minority rights in the republics of eastern Europe and in a classless society in the Soviet Union.

Added to all this was the fact that the joint campaign was not succeeding. Only $2.5 million had been pledged and only $1.5 million had been collected in a $6-million campaign.

It was, however, an amicable parting. The announcement stressed that "every endeavor would be made by both organizations so to conduct their campaigns as to keep intact the harmony, the mutual goodwill and cooperation which had been such important by-products of the Allied Jewish Campaign." To promote this harmonious relationship, the Committee on Campaign Relations was established.

Three years later, when a peril of unprecedented proportions confronted one of the world's leading Jewish communities, the Joint Distribution Committee and the American Palestine Campaign were ready to unite in joint fundraising. Hitler came to power in 1933; in March 1934 the United Jewish Appeal was created. It is significant that the new joint effort was termed "United" rather than "Allied." "Allied" implies that the individual components will retain the fullness of their individual identity and autonomy, and that the coming together is for a specific purpose limited by parochial interests and bounded by time. "United" connotes a new and separate entity, having its own identity and integrity, unlimited in duration. The intention foundered on the rocks of reality.

A campaign for $3.25 million was launched. By September 1935, only $1.5 million had been raised. A call by two hundred prominent non-Jews—bishops, deans of theological schools, university presidents, and political and civil leaders—was issued to little avail. By the end of October, the UJA's executive committee found it wisest to terminate the effort. Again, the announcement of dissolution pointed to the important benefits which had accrued to the American Jewish community through this united effort, but it had to admit that the campaign itself was a failure. It was recognized and stated that

> one of the advantages of separate campaigns was that both the Joint Distribution Committee and the American Palestine Campaign would be free to intensify their special appeals and could enlist in their particular efforts additional supporters for their respective programs in the field of European aid and reconstruction, and Palestine upbuilding.

It is important to note also that the statement of termination needed to say that the decision "does not preclude the possibility of joint local drives, on an optional basis, in such communities where a joint campaign may be regarded as advisable." There was greater unity and desire for united efforts in the local communities than in the national bodies.

The individual campaigns launched by both groups (the American Palestine Campaign now took the name United Palestine Appeal) proved successful. The UPA announced that in the first half of 1936 it raised sums larger than at any time since 1928, and the JDC boasted of pledges triple those of the year before. But despite the success of the individual campaigns the pressures for unified fundraising continued.

To relieve the pressures, each component body stressed that its field of interest and activity did not compete with or impinge upon the other. Both were needed and necessary. Thus the JDC emphasized that its work "will have to concentrate on bringing aid to the German and Polish Jews," and that it "feels justified in expecting other agencies to give [immigrant Jews] their start in Palestine." The UPA accepted this responsibility and pointed to the fact that increasing numbers of German and Polish Jews would be needing a new "start in Palestine."

But the force of American Jewish communal demands was for unity in the raising of the funds, not in their distribution. The manner in which the campaigns were organized and conducted affected local communal life, and the communities wanted the campaigns to be activities which would bring amity and unity. The issue was brought to a head in January 1937, when the Council of Jewish Federations and Welfare Funds initiated a series of consultations between representatives of the two organizations "with a view of promoting the fullest cooperation between them and of securing from local Jewish Welfare Funds the maximum response to their appeals." After a series of conferences, agreements were reached for the JDC to receive 60 percent, and the UPA 40 percent, of sums collected for them by local Jewish welfare funds. Both agencies would continue their separate existence and fundraising apparatus and activities, but they would give fullest cooperation to local campaigns. These arrangements marked the acceptance by the national relief agencies of a role in their fundraising by local federations. It presaged a united campaign and the increasing importance of the Council of Jewish Federations and Welfare Funds in the direction of the campaign.

The council, which by the late 1930s was beginning to be a body of considerable influence, emerged from a number of mergers of service bureaus designed to aid local federations in their programs of community coordination and fundraising. By the end of the nineteenth century most Jewish communities had central charitable associations. (Some had two such bodies, one of and for the German Jewish community, and another serving the eastern European.) During the last quarter of the century attempts had been made to establish a national organization, culminating in the creation of the National Conference of Jewish Charities, which later evolved into the National Conference for Jewish Communal Service, which, as the name implies, was a federation of independent local bodies to aid one another "without interfering with the local work of any constituent agency." The local community organizations, called federations, grew in number as communities became stabilized, reaching forty-two by the end of World War I. In 1927, the National Conference founded the National Appeals Information Service to secure and disseminate to its member federations "accurate information . . . about Jewish organizations making national appeals throughout the United States."

Almost a decade earlier the field bureau of the National Conference and the research department of the American Jewish Committee had merged to form the Bureau of Jewish Social Research. In 1932 the bureau urged the formation of a National Council of Jewish Federations and Welfare Funds, and three years later it merged into the council.

The mergers and consolidation reflect a community growing, stabilizing, assuming a sense of national communal identity. A pattern evolved which mirrors the American experience of nation building, the acceptance of a federated form of national unity. A high measure of independence and power was retained by the local bodies; from their strength the national body derived its power. To it the local entities delegated authority to deal with others. The council was thus empowered by its constituents to represent them in their relations with national Jewish bodies. Cognizant of the source of its power, the council was ever zealous of strengthening the local community federations. Realizing that the collectors of monies retain a measure of control over the funds they raise, and that such control confers influence and the power of decision, it worked at transferring major national Jewish fundraising to the federations. The 1937 agreement mentioned above was the first important step in that direction. The council made itself useful and, in time, indispensable to the federations by serving as their service agency in campaigning, and as their coordinating body in cooperation and confrontation with national Jewish agencies. Through its Large City Budgeting Council, it provided budgeting information, which became allocation advice, giving it considerable influence in directing the distribution of the monies raised, and arming it with powerful leverage in its dealings with others.

In 1937, however, it could act the "honest broker," not yet the "power broker." Despite the council's attempts to create fundraising unity, the JDC and UPA conducted their own independent campaigns. The 1938 campaign netted the JDC almost $1.5 million more than the year before.

Once again history intervened late that year to force unity of action upon American Jewry. On November 10, a country-wide pogrom swept through Nazi Germany. The broken glass of windows and showcases shattered by the Nazis gave it the name *Kristallnacht* ("crystal night"). Shops were looted, homes invaded, heads of families incarcerated. The most shocking of all was the desecrating, gutting, and burning of all the synagogues.

In Germany, the synagogue was more than a house of worship. To the German Jew, it was his statement of at-homeness in that land. Now this symbol lay shattered, as if the enemy now gave its visible expression that in the Thousand-Year Reich there was no place for the Jew.

For the American Jew it was as if his own synagogue had been violated. To him the synagogue was his portal to America, a symbol of his acceptance in and by America. The gutted synagogues of Germany were an affront to him, their charred ruins an evil omen. For in the 1930s the American Jew had experienced a new form of anti-Jewish agitation. Social bigotry and economic discrimination, which he had experienced and learned to cope with, was replaced by actions of uniformed Bundists and Silver Shirts, who had ties to and conjured up the strength of the virulent, powerful anti-Semitic movements of Europe.

The immediate response was a drawing together to strengthen one another and to aid those whom dark forces had already victimized. In January 1939, the Joint Distribution Committee, the United Palestine Appeal, and the National Coordinating Committee Fund (refugee aid) joined to form the United Jewish Appeal for Refugee and Overseas Needs, and announced a campaign for $20 million. The joint campaign realized over $15 million, whereas the separate campaigns a year earlier had only raised about $7 million.

As if to give symbolic answer to those who burned the synagogues, the campaign of a united American Jewry named as its cochairmen Abba Hillel Silver and Jonah B. Wise, two of America's most distinguished rabbis.

The United Jewish Appeal campaign of 1939 marked the culmination of a quarter of a century of nationally organized efforts on behalf of brethren. The campaigns had provided "bread for the hungry—shrouds for the dead." They helped communities reconstitute themselves in postwar Europe, and provided physical and cultural sustenance for Jews in need throughout the world. Colonization in the Soviet Union and the nation building in Palestine were its concerns and interests. The refugees from Nazi terror were its beneficiaries.

It was the period in which American Israel came of age. Over a million people were added to the population, bringing it close to five million, one-third of world Jewry. The community established a thousand new congregations, built synagogues and community centers, and trained the personnel to staff them. It devised strategies with which to confront bigotry and discrimination and fashioned agencies to employ them. A new imaging of America as a land of "cultural pluralism" replaced the "melting pot," and made the American Jew more comfortable in his cultural and religious otherness. It provided justification for Jewish cultural endeavor and creativity, and gave legitimacy to Zionist commitment and activities. Acceptance of fraternal responsibility for the well-being of brethren overseas conferred maturity; the response to the challenge it presented forged unity. At the period's beginning, the community was so divided that, whereas needs abroad could make for a unity in the distribution of funds through one agency, the Joint Distribution Committee, realities at home made it mandatory to raise these funds through three fundraising entities. At its end when the distributing agencies had become divided by ideological interests and historical commitments, one united campaign was willed by the community—the United Jewish Appeal. It took a traumatizing crisis abroad to force this unity, but the elements were ready and awaiting a catalyst.

The large-scale immigration was brought to an end by restrictive immigration laws in the early 1920s. An ever-larger percentage of the community was American born. Similarly, a growing homogeneity of language, culture, and occupational patterns was making for a natural unity. It was a community that was beginning to view ethnic differences and social divisions with suspicion. These were felt to be vestiges of a European experience which the free air of America should expunge. Freedom meant equality in the Jewish community as well as for it. America was moving toward a cultural climate characterized by sociologists as "ethnic assimilation and religious differentiation." Most American-born Jews hewed to that definition and willed that it be mirrored in the Jewish community. They had little patience for divisions along ethnic, social, or cultural lines. If diversity there would be, let it be that diversity which had always been most acceptable and "legitimate" in America—a religious diversity. But in all other matters, let there be unity, most especially in matters touching on the well-being of fellow Jews in need.

There were strong forces, ideological and organizational, which for reasons of policy or power thwarted the move to unity. The major national Jewish organizations were committed to diversity, and fought hard to retain their institutional integrity. The local community federations espoused unity. The first and easiest step toward unity was to join in aid of coreligionists in distress overseas. The United Jewish Appeal became a vehicle for that quest for unity.

III

WE
ARE
ONE

In the United States there remained the only important Jewish community in the world, operating within the framework of the democratic way of life, in a country still at peace.

—*American Jewish Year Book* (5700, 1939–1940)

Recent history has shown us that whenever he is forsaken by his own, the Jew is lost. But when he is supported by his own, he can begin again. Together, we share an extraordinary adventure, which with its joys and tears confers meaning on all of Jewish life.

—Elie Wiesel

10.

The United Jewish
Appeal: Beginnings

A "Review of the Year" for 5700 (July 1, 1939 to June 30, 1940) in the *American Jewish Year Book* states:

> The outbreak of the European war in September and the rapid extension of Nazi domination over the greater part of Europe, with its profound effect on Jewish life overseas, and its serious threats to democracy throughout the world, held the focus of attention of American Jewry during the period under review. In the United States there remained the only important Jewish community in the world operating within the framework of the democratic way of life, in a country still at peace. The rapid march of events abroad imposed upon American Jews the twofold responsibility of extending material aid and moral support on an unprecedented scale to the victims of Nazi war and persecution, and of strengthening the communal and cultural bases of Jewish life in America. . . . The effects of the war on Palestine held the attention of the American Jewish community which became practically the sole remaining source of moral and material support for the Jewish settlement there. . . .
>
> Above all, the necessity of caring for refugees and other victims of the war resulted in an unprecedented expansion of relief efforts. The United States became the center of Zionist efforts and assumed the leadership in Jewish life throughout the world.

It was in this atmosphere of crisis and peril abroad and heightened responsibility at home that the United Jewish Appeal was born. The results of the first campaign attested to both the efficacy of the union which brought the UJA into being and the effectiveness of the newborn agency. The $16 million raised in thirty-two hundred Jewish communities throughout the country was more than double that of the previous individual efforts. But the infant had no life of its own. Each year it had to be born anew through renegotiated agreement by the parent organizations. At the end of the 1940 campaign, which had secured pledges of some $14 million, the cochairmen, Rabbis Abba Hillel Silver and Jonah B. Wise, announced that "as of December 31, 1940, the United Jewish Appeal will cease to function as the agency for the collection and distribution of new funds for the 1941 programs of the Joint Distribution Committee, the United Palestine Appeal and the National Refugee Service."

The three constituents announced individual campaigns, but they had not properly assessed the mood of the Jewish community. Before the announcement of dissolution, the Council of Jewish Federations and Welfare Funds had attempted to mediate, but without success. But the announcement itself aroused such vigorous and vocal protest from leaders in every walk of life, and from communities in all parts of the country, that the constituent agencies thought it wise to reconsider. The General Assembly of the council, meeting in February 1941, served as a forum to discuss the unresolved issues: a proposed national advisory budgeting service and the needs of the National Refugee Service. But the overriding sentiment which found expression on the floor of the assembly was an opposition to dissolution and a call to a return to unity. Within a month, issues were resolved and an agreement to reconstitute the UJA was reached. The announced goal was $25 million. Of the first $8 million raised the JDC would receive $4.275 million, the UPA $2.525 million, the NRS $2 million. The balance of the funds would be allocated by an allotment committee as had been done in 1940.

What became increasingly obvious was that the power of decision was moving from the national agencies to the local communities; that those who raised the funds would have increasing voice in how this would be done; that the campaign apparatus would have influence on the distribution; that the council provided the forum for community expression but was not the vehicle for it; and that the United Jewish Appeal was being willed a life of its own not by the agencies which begat it, but by the communities which used it and in the process were united by it.

A Report to American Jews—On Overseas Relief, Palestine and Refugees in the United States, prepared by Eli Ginsberg, director of research for the 1941 allotment committee of the UJA, disclosed that approximately $40 million had been raised in the three years of its existence, but concluded that there was a wide gap between the potential ability of American Jews to support overseas relief work and the rebuilding of Palestine, and their actual contributions to the United Jewish Appeal. The report maintained that a large proportion of Jews representing all income classes gave nothing at all or only a modicum of what they could have contributed.

This was the first "scientific" argument, made by an expert economist, that American Jewry could contribute far more than it was doing. It issued a challenge to the community to look to the seriousness of its commitment and to the genuineness of its generosity. It was an argument and challenge which would be heard again and again.

November 1942 marked a turning point in the fortunes of war for the Allied armies. They made an initial breach in the Nazi lines, and were soon able to liberate North Africa and parts of Italy. The push eastward continued, and the process of liberation of Nazi-enslaved countries was on the way. The prospects of peace abroad seemed to permit contention at home. Ideological and practical conflicts came to the fore. Most pronounced was the Zionist/anti-Zionist confrontation.

In preparation for a postwar world, and the place of Jews within it, the American Jewish Committee adopted a position paper. The paper expressed approval of and appreciation for the growth of Jewish settlement in Palestine but stated that such settlement "cannot alone furnish and should not be expected to furnish the solution of the problem of postwar Jewish rehabilitation." It argued that "there should be no preconceived formula at this time as to the permanent political structure which shall obtain there." It called for an international trusteeship under the United Nations to safeguard Jewish settlement in and Jewish immigration to Palestine "to the full extent of the economic absorptive capacity of a self-governing commonwealth under a constitution and bill of rights that will safeguard and protect these purposes and basic rights for all."

The Zionists termed this an anti-Zionist position and argued that it made negotiations for joint action impossible. Others argued that it left sufficient room for cooperation if not agreement between Zionists and non-Zionists. Among these was Henry Monsky, first president of the B'nai B'rith to have come from the eastern European Jewish community. Under his leadership a call went out for the convening of an American Jewish Assembly "to establish a common program of action in connection with postwar problems." One of three items on the agenda was "the implementation of the rights of the Jewish people with respect to Palestine." It had a definite Zionist ring to it, so both the American Jewish Committee and the Jewish Labor Committee absented themselves from the convening meeting. (As we have seen, after long negotiations both agreed to participate in an American Jewish Conference.)

The anti-Zionist forces, led by ninety Reform rabbis and some prominent laymen, formed the American Council for Judaism to oppose Jewish nationalism and the establishment of a Jewish state in Palestine.

GREAT DAY. Hundreds of children, vanguard of the 100,000 homeless European Jews who this year will enter Israel through your support of the $250,000,000 United Jewish Appeal, shown as they arrived at Haifa recently aboard the S.S. Negbah. This is the chance they waited for. We gave it to them.

Journey's End — Home in Israel

This is their year, and ours—a 'Year of Opportunity' for us, a 'Year of Fulfilment' for them.

This is their year to leave the DP camps behind them forever. This is their year to go to Israel, to go home for good. This is their year to enter a new era of peace, dignity, freedom and independence.

This is our year—our year to make all this possible for *them*. This is our year, through our support of the $250,000,000 United Jewish Appeal, to enable the Joint Distribution Committee, United Palestine Appeal and United Service for New Americans *to give them the chance they need*.

THEY ASK FOR A <u>CHANCE</u> TO LIVE IN A TIN HUT...

...But it must be in Israel

WHAT WILL TOMORROW BRING FOR THEM? Can she dare hope that she'll leave Iraq with her child on the next plane to Israel? Only your help can answer the unspoken question in her eyes.

They're modest and reasonable, the hopes of these newcomers. At this moment a tin hut with a table and cots and a primus stove would be a mansion to them . . . if it's in Israel.

They're ready to work, to build permanent homes, tilling fields and irrigating the land to increase the yield of Israel's agriculture to meet food shortages. They are eager for the chance to start living as decent human beings in a free country. Yes, a hut is enough—provided it's a haven in a land they can call their own.

But for 100,000 waiting in areas of dangerous tension for rescue planes and ships to take them to Israel, the margin of time is narrowing. July 31 is the final date for rescuing them. And another 100,000 must reach Israel before the year is out.

So, it won't even be a tin hut if desperately needed cash isn't available in time to bring them to Israel. There's no knowing where they'll have to stay tomorrow if we should fail them.

We can save them now, set them on the road to useful lives in work camps first, and then, permanently, in settlements. But cash is needed to get them there; to care for them on arrival; to build 20,000 temporary housing units to shelter them.

Cash is needed to continue the life-saving programs of the United Jewish Appeal through its member agencies, the United Palestine Appeal, Joint Distribution Committee and United Service for New Americans.

They ask so little—but it means so much. You can give them the chance to start living now. Give generously. Give cash.

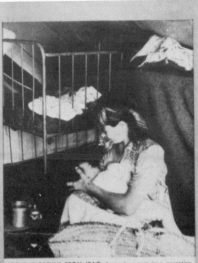

THEY'RE HOME! This family waited long and anxiously in Eastern Europe for this moment, when UJA funds have made it possible for them to start a new life in Israel.

FOR THIS FAMILY FROM IRAQ, home is a tent in a reception camp. Your support of the 1951 United Jewish Appeal can make it possible for them to live in a house with walls and a roof.

IT'S THE FREE SOIL OF ISRAEL, and he tills it proudly. Behind him, his home—a tin hut. It's modest, but it's a beginning.

IT'S CROWDED, but it's home for this group of newcomers who were rescued in time from Iraq by the UJA-financed airlift. Thousands of others still wait, but you can help save them. Cash is needed to transport them, house them, care for them in Israel, now.

The Council of Jewish Federations was powerless to mediate between the contending forces. It could not even carry out the mandate of the local communities for the integration of the programs of the four leading defense agencies.

The issue even divided families. In the year in which Lessing Rosenwald founded the American Council for Judaism, his brother William served as a cochairman of the United Jewish Appeal. Both brothers had inherited their father's generosity, but one also inherited his opposition to Zionism while the other inherited his commitment to *noblesse oblige* participation in Jewish community affairs, beyond ideological confinement.

It was in such an atmosphere of community tensions that the United Jewish Appeal had to operate. It alone brought a needed unity to a community which had become the largest in the Jewish world, and the only one to whom the Jews of a wartorn world could look for "material aid and moral support."

In 1944, President Roosevelt expressed wholehearted approval of the efforts of the UJA, calling it "one of the agencies through which the American people can make their contribution to the fight for decency, human dignity and freedom for all to live." The UJA set its quota for that year at $32 million, and issued a call to the Jewish community:

> In 1944, the Jews in the United States will be confronted with a dual challenge—that of saving from destruction large numbers of victims still in the grip of oppression and enlarging the tasks of reconstruction for those who have already been liberated by the Allied armies.

Within the first six months over $20 million was disbursed by the constituent agencies. By year's end, over $27 million was raised. The JDC continued to get the larger share of the funds, but the gap was narrowing. The general formula was that after an initial small grant to the NRS, 57 percent would go to the JDC and 42 percent to the UPA, but the arrangements varied from year to year, and reflected the changing condition and needs of the beneficiaries.

In the first thirty years of its operation, the JDC "disbursed a total of $142 million for overseas relief, rescue and rehabilitation." Reviewing the 1939–1944 period, Joseph J. Schwartz, head of European operations for the JDC in those years, wrote in 1955:

> During these five years of war and Nazi persecution, 5,814,000 European Jews perished in gas chambers, in slave-labor camps, in ghettos and during deportation. But the survival of 1,430,000 Jews in Western, Central and Eastern Europe (excluding the Soviet Union), was, to more than a modest degree, the result of the life-saving mission of the Joint Distribution Committee. Operating in Portugal, Switzerland and Turkey, JDC untiringly provided aid through various channels, including diplomatic missions in neutral countries and the underground. . . . In spite of numerous obstacles and perilous conditions prevailing in German-occupied Europe, the JDC and the Jewish Agency were able to rescue 162,000 Jews from *Festung Europa* during 1939–1944 of whom 50,000 were brought to Palestine. . . .
>
> As the World War II hostilities expanded and became literally global, so did the life-saving work supported by UJA.
>
> At the end of 1944, UJA funds provided relief to distressed Jews in forty-eight countries: seventeen in Europe; eleven in Arab and Middle Eastern lands; seventeen in Central and South America and three elsewhere.

11.

1946: A Year of Testing and Triumph

The first postwar National Conference of the United Jewish Appeal for Refugees, Overseas Needs and Palestine was held in Atlantic City on December 15–17, 1945. It was the most representative assembly of American Jewry ever gathered. The participants were weighted with the knowledge that fewer than one and a half million were now left of the once-great European Jewish community. In September of that year, President Truman had released the "Harrison Report," the findings of a special investigation on the condition of the Jewish Displaced Persons in the American Occupied Zone of Germany. On the basis of his findings, Earl G. Harrison, American member of the Intergovernmental Committee on Refugees, recommended that a hundred thousand DP's be permitted to immigrate to British Mandated Palestine, whose gates had been shut to Jews seeking asylum. Survivors of the death camps confronted the conference with their plea and challenge. In response, the assembled leaders of America's Jews unanimously voted to undertake a campaign for $100 million.

That $100 million was three times as much as had been raised the year before and almost four times the figure of the year

previous. It was an unprecedented, bold step. The leadership of
the UJA had carefully prepared to make it a responsible one.

Since the creation of the UJA, it had been directed by a duo of
executives and a trio of national chairmen. The professionals
were Isidor Coons of the JDC and Henry Montor of the UPA. A
co-worker described Coons as "a very steady, quiet person, a
man of great ability," while Montor appeared as "a very
dynamic personality . . . the two were equal excepting Mr.
Montor was always more equal." The $100-million goal was
the decision of Montor. "Everybody said Montor was crazy,
including his leadership," a campaign worker recalled.

William Rosenwald was a national cochairman of the campaign beginning in 1942. His retelling of the fateful decision is
worth recording:

> Henry Montor, who was the active director of the campaign, felt
> that he could raise $100 million. I didn't think he could, but I
> thought we should set the $100 million as a *goal,* a goal. At that
> time the Joint Distribution Committee got a larger share than the
> United Palestine Appeal. So with this in mind, I went to the
> Executive Committee of the JDC, a small group, and urged them
> to accept the $100 million goal. . . . The feeling of the Executive
> Committee was very strong that there wasn't a chance of raising
> $100 million. Moreover, they were afraid such an exaggerated
> goal would destroy the usefulness of future goals. . . . They
> thought it would be a miracle if we raised $70 million. The
> situation in Europe was really desperate with millions of Jews
> who had lost everything: their health, their families—
> everything. . . . So I said you must try for it, and it was passed at
> the Executive by a vote of *one to nothing.* I voted for it and
> nobody would vote against me.

Mr. Rosenwald had the ability to back up his conviction and
decision. Before going to the preliminary campaign meeting in
Atlantic City, he had arranged with his sisters to give a million
dollars. At the meeting, a few top professionals from larger
cities and a few top lay leaders were discussing the feasibility of
a $100-million goal and somebody said, "Impossible." Mr.

Rosenwald said, "My family is prepared to give a million dollars." From then on everybody took the $100-million goal for granted.

Thirty years earlier the million-dollar gift of Julius Rosenwald drove American Jewry to new heights of commitment and generosity; his posthumous reward was that, three decades later, his children's gift did the same.

To set a goal is to declare a commitment. But the most sincerely stated commitments are the most difficult to accomplish, for sincerity propels one to the limits of his devotion. The electric atmosphere of Atlantic City, created by the dramatic appearances of the DP's and the challenging Rosenwald gift, did not follow the communal leaders back to their communities. It was a long, arduous task to get community after community to accept its allocated quota. A veteran UJA professional, Sam Abramson, remembers:

> You had to go in and get them to accept it and they had to raise it. I remember going to some communities and having battles and coming back. They wouldn't accept the whole quota, so I had to go back and reopen the whole thing. . . . Of course, the $100 million was exceeded.

The vision and the daring of Henry Montor was vindicated, as was his assessment of the philanthropic capacity of the American Jewish community. The success of the campaign established the hegemony of the UJA in the postwar American Jewish community. Seven years earlier, the communities forced a united campaign upon the founding agencies; now the UJA imposed its demands on the communities. In each case the Jewish situation abroad was the determining factor.

The 1947 campaign raised nearly $150 million, and the campaign of the year of Israeli statehood more than $200 million. Montor continued to be architect and builder of the effort. He enlisted Henry Morgenthau, Jr., former secretary of the treasury in the Roosevelt cabinet, to serve as national chairman.

In the following years the sums fell off. The headlines were no longer quite so black, and the euphoria of witnessing the fulfillment of a two-millennial dream, the establishment of a Jewish state, abated. Montor engaged in confrontations with local welfare funds and the Council of Jewish Federations and Welfare Funds. Funds collected by the appeal of the UJA, he accused, were being used for local needs. At times the confrontation led to threats of UJA campaigns independent of the local federations, but compromise made possible the continuation of the union between federation and the UJA—a marriage which was kept alive by shared common interests, and, like all good marriages, was mutually demanding and mutually rewarding. The UJA gained a ready-made apparatus for fundraising; the federations were provided with a cause which raised campaign sums far beyond what local and national causes could have elicited.

Prof. Salo Baron, reviewing the period of 1946–1947, writes:

> In the United States alone, they [the Jews] could venture to undertake a campaign to raise $170 million for the United Jewish Appeal. This undertaking, unprecedented even in the glorious annals of Jewish communal welfare, was superimposed upon many national and local campaigns, for schools of higher learning, local federations, etc. . . . Nor was there any evidence that the tremendous charitable and educational expenditures entailed any serious personal hardships to the majority of contributors.

It may be noted that in 1947 6 percent of the contributors (giving $500 and over) were the source of 75 percent of the funds raised. A campaign dependent to so large a measure on a small number of contributors has a degree of tension and volatility built in. That the UJA has attained such a solid record of stability, so as to be considered a system of voluntary but expected taxation, is testimony to its basic and ongoing appeal, an appeal which provides continuing motivation and mandates communal unity as well.

The unprecedented giving to the 1946 campaign, both in size of contributions and numbers of gifts, ushered in a new era in American Jewish philanthropic endeavor. It demonstrated the capacity of the American Jew to give, and his readiness to do so under the proper motivation. Other charitable enterprises took heart and lesson. Institutions of religion and culture found that having given to one cause, the donor was easier to solicit for another. The new standard of giving was a gift of the great campaign to American Jewish communal life and institutions.

12.

Eyes Toward Zion

The establishment of the State of Israel had its impact on the fortunes of the UJA. Anticipation evokes greater enthusiasm than realization. The state established, there was a serious falling off in sums realized, decreasing by 30 percent in 1949. The formula of distribution was also affected. Heretofore, the JDC had been, as we have seen, the major recipient. Now, however, the precampaign agreement provided that of the first $50 million, 40 percent would go to the JDC and 60 percent to the UPA. Of the next $25 million, the allotment was 30 and 70 percent, and beyond that, 25 and 75 percent. Clearly the center of Jewish concern and the object of its philanthropy had shifted to the Jewish community in Israel.

It was also found that just as the chief beneficiary during periods of growing contributions was the UJA, now, when the amount was declining, it became the chief sufferer. In order to assure itself its due share of the local campaigns, the UJA adopted a policy of "precampaign budgeting." Since it was generally conceded that the campaigns depended for their success on the appeal of the UJA causes, communities were persuaded to guarantee a minimum percentage which the UJA would receive. One can well imagine that the negotiations

—————————— An Editorial ——————————

Test of Friendship
By T. O. THACKREY

On Saturday 1200 United States citizens will assemble at the Shoreham in Washington to launch officially the $250,000,000 campaign for funds urgently needed in 1949 if the promise of Israel is to be fulfilled.

The funds are needed for mass migration and settlement in Israel, rehabilitation in Europe and North Africa and refugee adjustment in the United States. The United Palestine Appeal, the Joint Distribution Committee, and the United Service for New Americans are the principal agencies charged with those responsibilities.

Specifically the objectives of the 1949 campaign are stated by Henry Morgenthau Jr., U.J.A. general chairman, as follows:

1. Emptying the D.P. camps where some 75,000 Jewish refugees still wait for a new home.

2. Immigration into Israel of 250,000 homeless Jews this year from the D.P. centers, Eastern Europe and North Africa. Presently the immigration rate is approximately 25,000 per month.

3. Reception, care, housing, health and medical care and retraining of refugess. More than 40,000 newcomers in Israel are living in reception-camps and thousands in tents. But if the rate of immigration should slow down, the opportunity for emigration from many European centers will have been lost, either by fiat or by death.

4. Establishment of new agricultural settlements in the Negeb, the Jerusalem corridor and in Galilee.

5. Increased assistance for the hundreds of thousands of Jews remaining in Europe and Africa.

6. Support of reconstruction in European countries where Jewish communities are beginning to recover normal integration into the broader community.

7. Adjustment of 25,000 Jewish refugees expected to reach the United States in 1949, if the present Displaced Persons act is liberalized.

American generosity is needed to support "the greatest homecoming of all history," which can be brought through to a successful conclusion only if all who value freedom and liberty give of their time, strength and money.

Peace is yet to be won.

No official act, no diplomatic or State Department representation is required to influence the result of the U.J.A. campaign.

Only you, and I, can do that.

"This effort can be brought through to a successful conclusion only if all who value freedom and liberty give of their time, strength and money . . . ."

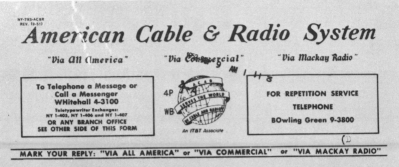

American Cable & Radio System

"Via All America"   *"Via Commercial"*   *"Via Mackay Radio"*

To Telephone a Message or
Call a Messenger
WHitehall 4-3100
Teletypewriter Exchanges:
NY 1-405, NY 1-406 and NY 1-407
OR ANY BRANCH OFFICE
SEE OTHER SIDE OF THIS FORM

4P
WB

An IT&T Associate

FOR REPETITION SERVICE
TELEPHONE
BOwling Green 9-3800

MARK YOUR REPLY: "VIA ALL AMERICA" or "VIA COMMERCIAL" or "VIA MACKAY RADIO"

JERUSALEM SEPT 9

EMM WARBURG UJAPPEAL NEW YORK

MY VISIT TO ISRAEL HAS SHOWN ME THRILLING
PROOF OF NATIONS PROGRESS IN PAST YEAR BUT
I HAVE ALSO WITNESSED CONTINUING HARDSHIPS
WHICH PEOPLE BEAR STOP PRIME MINISTER
BEN GURION TOLD ME TODAY THAT ISRAEL FACES
DESPERATE SHORTAGE OF DOLLARS STOP BECAUSE
ISRAEL LACKS HARD CURRENCY SOME TWO HUNDRED
AND FORTY THOUSAND PERSONS MUST STILL LIVE
IN TENTS AND FLIMSY SHACKS STOP WINTER CUTS
IN FOOD RATIONS EXPECTED STOP RAW MATERIALS
IMPORTS SLASHED THEREBY THREATENING CRISIS
IN PRODUCTION VITAL FOR FOREIGN TRADE STOP
FURTHER DRAINS ON PRECIOUS FOREIGN EXCHANGE
RESERVE NECESSARY BECAUSE ISRAEL CANNOT
RELAX DEFENSE PRECAUTIONS AMID CONTINUING
NEAR EAST POLITICAL TURMOIL STOP DEEPLY
IMPRESSED BY NECESSITY TO RAISE CASH QUICKLY
FEEL COMPELLED TO ACCEPT YOUR REQUEST THAT
I SERVE AS CHAIRMAN OF UNITED JEWISH APPEAL
CASH CAMPAIGN FOR THIRTY FIVE MILLION
DOLLARS STOP SITUATION DEMANDS ALL AMERICAN
JEWISH COMMUNITIES BE MOBILIZED FOR INTENSIVE
EFFORT STOP RETURNING IMMEDIATELY TO UNITED
STATES TO GET CASH CAMPAIGN UNDER WAY

JACK WEILER

brought on tensions and occasional confrontations. But even on so volatile an issue as this, the basic integrity of the cooperative campaign structure was maintained. Montor, however, continued to inveigh that the local institutions and organizations were receiving funds which rightly should have gone to Israel: "Since the overwhelming bulk of Jews gave to Israel, therefore, the overwhelming bulk of the funds should go for Israel, and not be stripped away for other purposes, however valid they may be." Montor later recalled:

> This, of course, meant an annual battle with every major Jewish community in America. . . . We had a meeting with the budget committee of the Jewish Welfare Fund of Chicago in 1948. . . . The antagonism was very sharp to the figure I had cited. . . . "If Chicago does not feel that it can give that money, then my proposal is that we separate ourselves from the Jewish Welfare Fund and set up a refugee camp on the outskirts of Chicago. The Jews can come and see how refugees live in Europe, so that they can thus be inspired to do something more adequate for the amelioration of their condition and their placement in Israel." . . . But eventually we came to a compromise.

Confrontations leave their wounds and a point is reached beyond which "victories" become counterproductive. The place of the UJA on the American Jewish communal landscape had been firmly established by Montor's creative utilization of American Jewry's response to the plight of brethren, and by his own resolute will. What he was fighting for now was for maximum possible aid for the displaced Jews of Europe who had found haven and home in the ancient homeland born anew. In service of that cause, he created a new outlet for the utilization of his unusual ability to persuade, initiate, launch, and establish.

On September 3–6, 1950, fifty-nine leaders of American Jewry met with Prime Minister David Ben-Gurion in Jerusalem "to consider the economic situation of Israel." They called for private investment in Israel, for the continuation of the United

Jewish Appeal "on an enlarged scale to elicit the widest possible response," and for a pledge that "should the Government of Israel decide to float a public loan ... American Jewry will extend its fullest support."

What grew out of that pledge was the American Financial and Development Corporation for Israel, later called the Israel Bonds Organization. To launch it in May 1951, Ben-Gurion came to the United States, his only trip outside Israel during his first term as prime minister. Henry Morgenthau, Jr., arranged U.S. governmental approval and moved over from chairmanship of the UJA to head the bonds effort. Henry Montor, who promoted and organized the project, left the UJA to launch it and take it through its first years.

13.

1947–1950: Years of Rescue and Return

The dramatically successful campaign of 1946, which broke through the "$100-million barrier," established the power and independence of the United Jewish Appeal and solidified the professional leadership of Henry Montor. It was the last campaign headed by three cochairmen representing the Joint Distribution Committee, the United Palestine Appeal, and the National Refugee Service. Beginning in 1947, *one* national chairman symbolized not only the unity which the UJA had effected, but its independence as well.

The first to serve was Henry Morgenthau, Jr. He brought to it a long and distinguished career of public service, including more than a decade as secretary of the treasury in the cabinet of President Franklin Delano Roosevelt, the third-highest office in the land. During the war years, the plight of European Jewry had evoked his concern. In 1943 he persuaded Secretary of State Cordell Hull to permit the transfer of private U.S. funds to Europe to aid in the rescue of French and Roumanian Jews, and a year later he recommended to Roosevelt the establishment of the War Refugee Board. The devastation brought upon Europe by the Nazi war machine caused him to propose a peace plan which would have turned Germany into an agrarian land. After the war, the plight of the remnant of his people in war-devastated Europe turned his energies and influence to their service. From 1947 to 1950 he served as general chairman of the UJA, and in a similar capacity for Bonds for Israel in 1950–1954.

Morgenthau came to Jewish causes late in life. "Montor must have conditioned a good deal of his thinking because he came in more or less as a stranger to Jewish life and to Jewish community activity, and Montor had to teach him a lot of things, a lot of facts of life about the Jewish community and how it functions," Israel Goldstein, a veteran American Jewish leader, recalls, "but after that process of initial learning of what was going on, Morgenthau was in a position to form his own judgments and did so." Dr. Goldstein continues:

> He was a man of convictions, and once he came to his conclusions he stuck by them. He was very, very helpful to the United Jewish Appeal, not only because of the prestige he brought to it, but also because of the understanding he brought to it. Golda Meir's campaign for the UJA in 1948, which raised the largest amount . . . up to that time, was due in no small measure to the fact that Morgenthau appreciated her coming, understood what it was all about, and exercised his own independent . . . enthusiasm in winning for her the broadest possible hearing on the part of the American Jewish community.

What the UJA did for Morgenthau it did for a great number of American Jews in all walks of life. It directed their attention to a Jewish cause; it aroused their concern for the welfare of fellow Jews; and it offered them a vehicle for entry into Jewish communal life and activities. For very many, the door opened by the UJA led into lifelong participation in a wide variety of Jewish organizational and institutional enterprises.

The prestige Morgenthau brought to the cause was vital at that time. Those were the postwar years of heightened patriotic sentiments, intensified by the beginnings of the Cold War confrontation. The national security of the United States was uppermost in the minds and concerns of a significant number of America's most influential Jews. There were some who feared that the constituent agencies of the UJA had stepped beyond the boundaries of philanthropic activity and were engaged in political activity which might not be consonant with the national interests of the United States, now seeking allies in Europe and the Near East. Others, of anti-Zionist sentiments, opposed aid for a "foreign state," Israel. And there were those who questioned the wisdom of sending such large sums of money overseas.

Morgenthau had attained the highest office ever held by a Jew. He retained friendships with those wielding national power. His own commitment and enthusiasm provided a quasi-governmental approval for what the UJA and its component agencies were doing. Just as his father had put aside his anti-Zionism a generation earlier to come to the aid of coreligionists in need, his son could now rise above ideological considerations in service of the pitiful remnant of his people now seeking relocation and rehabilitation. He thus set an example to others to liberate themselves from ideological constriction and raise themselves to that enlightened compassion which would aid another to find life and hope "where it seemeth best to him." To all, his labors for the UJA said that this is the cause of highest priority, worthy of every Jew's utmost expenditure of time and substance and exertion of energies and passions.

During the Montor/Morgenthau era, the center of philanthropic concern was shifted from Europe to Israel. This made the involvement of non-Zionists in the leadership of the campaign all the more important. Morgenthau's presence made its contribution, but even more vital were the skills of Henry Montor. His career had been with the United Palestine Appeal, where he rose from public relations work to executive leadership. As the UPA man in the United Jewish Appeal he could subordinate ideological considerations to service of the cause at hand and still retain the enthusiastic support of the Zionists. To

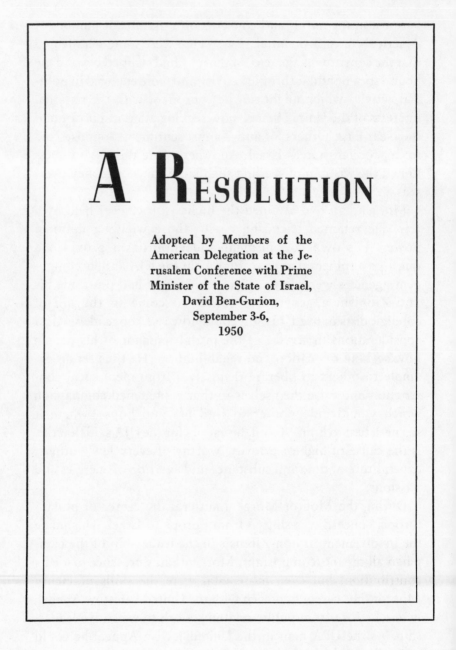

A Resolution

Adopted by Members of the
American Delegation at the Je-
rusalem Conference with Prime
Minister of the State of Israel,
David Ben-Gurion,
September 3-6,
1950

Meeting in the Holy City of Jerusalem, in the free and democratic State of Israel, which has admitted more than 450,000 homeless Jews in the last two years, and which has triumphed against all dangers and difficulties in establishing its independence, we, the fifty members of the delegation from the United States invited by Prime Minister David Ben-Gurion and by Berl Locker, Chairman of the Executive of the Jewish Agency, have been privileged to meet with the Prime Minister and other members of the Government to consider the economic situation of Israel and a three-year program for the development of the country.

After a comprehensive and frank discussion, we have arrived at the following conclusions:

1. That the people of Israel are dedicated to keep the doors wide open for all the hundreds of thousands of Jews fleeing from persecution and misery; and that they are ready to make every sacrifice to preserve the democratic way of life which is the moral essence of their very existence and that Israel is striving for peace so that it may give the full benefits of a free and productive life to all its people.

2. We have come to realize that the full magnitude of the tasks of absorbing hundreds of thousands of new immigrants in Israel and consolidating its economy on a sound basis is far beyond any conception which the Jews of America have so far entertained, and calls for a new approach to the scope of the cooperation between the Jews of the United States and the people of Israel.

3. In the light of the tremendous achievements already made in rehabilitating the land and developing industrial activities, we are confident that if the tools and capital are made available Israel will not only become self-supporting, but it will also serve as a dynamic and democratic force in the development of the entire Middle East.

4. The interest of American Jews in the future of Israel has been manifested by a high degree of generosity, and the flow of contributions to the United Jewish Appeal has made possible the outstanding accomplishments in mass immigration and settlement. However, the State of Israel has reached a crucial point of development in which contributions are not

adequate to meet long-range economic needs, and the Jews of America must recognize that new methods must be found to provide the far larger resources required in this vital transition period.

Far above the needs of financing this immigration is the program of complete absorption of many of those who have reached Israel in the past two years, and the hundreds of thousands who are expected to come in the next three years. To make this vast number of newcomers fully productive and integrate them into the economy of the country, Israel will require $1,500,000,000 for the next three years. The people of Israel are ready to make the utmost sacrifice to assume the fullest share of this responsibility. But $1,000,000,000 must come from the United States. Requirements of such scope cannot be provided in full through voluntary contributions alone, and consequently additional channels must be found to discharge this obligation.

Therefore we believe

a. That the United Jewish Appeal must be continued on an enlarged scale to elicit the widest possible response.

b. That should the Government of Israel decide to float a public loan in the United States as a means of obtaining funds for the financing of constructive programs, American Jewry will extend its fullest support and we pledge ourselves to render maximum service in the attainment of this objective.

c. There are many opportunities for private investment in Israel in productive and profitable projects. To realize the potentials in the field of private investment, more intensive efforts should be undertaken both in the United States and Israel.

Appreciating that this exploratory conference between American and Israel leaders will be productive to the degree that all of American Jewry will share in its conclusions, we of America urge the convening in the United States, at the earliest possible date, of a fully representative, national conference of the Jews of America, at which the conclusions reached here may be presented for the understanding and sanction of American Jewry, so that, with full knowledge and determination, it may go forward in accomplishing the most constructive enterprise in the history of our people.

Members of the American Delegation at the Jerusalem Conference with Prime Minister of the State of Israel, David Ben-Gurion, September 3-6, 1950

Herbert Abeles, *Newark, N. J.*
Martin Abelove, *Utica, N. Y.*
George Backer, *New York, N. Y.*
Henry C. Bernstein, *New York, N. Y.*
Leo Bernstein, *New York, N. Y.*
Philip Bernstein, *New York, N. Y.*
Maurice Boukstein, *New York, N. Y.*
Mrs. S. A. Brailove, *Elizabeth, N. J.*
Otto Bresky, *Boston, Mass.*
Benjamin G. Browdy, *New York, N. Y.*
Abraham Dickenstein, *New York, N. Y.*
Mrs. Katharine S. Falk, *New York, N. Y.*
Abraham Feinberg, *New York, N. Y.*
Prof. Haym Fineman, *Philadelphia, Pa.*
Julian Freeman, *Indianapolis, Ind.*
Rabbi Herbert Friedman, *Denver, Colo.*
Dr. Nahum Goldmann, *New York, N. Y.*
Monroe Goldwater, *New York, N. Y.*
Sidney Green, *New York, N. Y.*
Mrs. Rose Halprin, *New York, N. Y.*
Gottlieb Hammer, *New York, N. Y.*
Joseph M. Hoodin, *Cincinnati, Ohio*
A. S. Kay, *Washington, D. C.*
Rabbi Max Kirshblum, *New York, N. Y.*
Moses A. Leavitt, *New York, N. Y.*
Dr. Harris Levine, *New York, N. Y.*
Harold F. Linder, *New York, N. Y.*
Louis Lipsky, *New York, N. Y.*
Mrs. Jeanette Lourie, *New York, N. Y.*

Philip W. Lown, *Auburn, Me.*
Boris Margolin, *New York, N. Y.*
Joseph Meyerhoff, *Baltimore, Md.*
Edward Mitchell, *Los Angeles, Calif.*
Fred Monosson, *Boston, Mass.*
Henry Montor, *New York, N. Y.*
Louis S. Myers, *Kansas City, Mo.*
Stanley C. Myers, *Miami, Fla.*
Robert R. Nathan, *Washington, D. C.*
Dr. Emanuel Neumann, *New York, N. Y.*
Irving Norry, *Rochester, N. Y.*
Oscar Pattiz, *Los Angeles, Calif.*
Ellis Radinsky, *New York, N. Y.*
Adolf Robison, *West Englewood, N. J.*
Samuel Rothberg, *Peoria, Ill.*
Judge Morris Rothenberg *
Joseph Schechtman, *New York, N. Y.*
Albert Schiff, *Columbus, Ohio*
Robert W. Schiff, *Columbus, Ohio*
Dr. Joseph J. Schwartz, *New York, N. Y.*
Harry Seeve, *New York, N. Y.*
Nathan Shainberg, *Memphis, Tenn.*
Morris Shapiro, *Boston, Mass.*
Joseph Shulman, *Paterson, N. J.*
Rudolf G. Sonneborn, *New York, N. Y.*
M. F. Steinglass, *New York, N. Y.*
Julian B. Venezky, *Peoria, Ill.*
Ralph Wechsler, *Newark, N. J.*
Meyer W. Weisgal, *New York, N. Y.*
Baruch Zuckerman, *New York, N. Y.*

* Deceased

him, *the* cause was the rescue and rehabilitation of *Sheerit Hapleta,* the surviving remnant of European Jewry. It was clear to him that rehabilitation could only be in Palestine, constituted as an independent Jewish state. American Jewry was now afforded the opportunity—which it must accept as a duty—to make possible the relocation of the remnant to that state, and to help it reestablish itself upon the land. This was the historic mandate to American Jewry. He saw it not as the prime, but as the only priority.

His service to the cause was single-minded, with all the power and problems that single-mindedness produces. But hindsight vindicates his assessment of the situation and his unrelenting pursuit of its solution. As a man trained in public relations, he knew how to tell the story, and tell it dramatically. He understood the power of the human longing for the vicarious experience of daring ventures. To American Jewry he offered the opportunity to give new life and new hope to a community that had known death. The power to revive a people was available on a pledge card. He had the gift of projecting an intensity into the project at hand which made all other matters seem pale in comparison. The legendary David A. Brown had brought drama into American Jewish fundraising during the 1920s. Montor adopted his techniques and went beyond them. His threat to a reluctant Chicago leadership to erect a tent-city of refugees in their midst made real the plight of these refugees and brought into sharp focus the contrast between their condition and that of those now being solicited to share a small part of their good fortune with the less fortunate.

To the dramatic appeals which he orchestrated, he also brought the organizational and operational techniques first fashioned by Joseph Willen of the Federation of Jewish Philanthropies of New York: organization by localities, professions, *landsmanshaften;* precampaign pledging; parlor meetings, card calling. But above all Montor brought to the campaign a vision of the potential of the American Jewish community, which no one dared imagine, much less announce. Then, having convinced his leadership to permit him to challenge the community with his perception of its potential, he organized and drove the campaign apparatus to make that potential actual. A laconic statement in the *American Jewish Year Book* for 1951 tells the story:

> Other cities [i.e., other than New York] saw a decline from the peak year of 1948 of 21 per cent in 1949 and 14 per cent in 1950. The sums raised in 1950 represented a decline of 32 per cent from 1948 but were still nearly triple the amount raised in 1945, the last year before the intensification of post-war fund raising began.

To be sure, history played its role: the Holocaust, the plight of the surviving remnant, the establishment of the State of Israel. But history is a neutral force. It needs to be confronted and utilized. This the United Jewish Appeal was able to do in the fateful postwar years—in the saving of survivors, in the reconstitution of a nation.

14.

In and with the Communities

In the nineteenth century, Jewish homes throughout the world had a charity box for the Jews of the Holy Land, the *Meir Ba'al Hanes pushke*. Before lighting Sabbath or holiday candles, for thanksgiving or in celebration, a Jew would drop a copper in the box. The monies would be periodically collected and sent to Palestine for the support of a large segment of the Jewish population who looked to this charity for its sustenance.

In 1888, in response to a query from Jeruham Zvi Kantrowitz, "chief officer of the Council of all Kolelim in New York," Rabbi Isaac Elchanan Spektor of Kovno, leading rabbinic authority of eastern European Jewry, forbade the use of charity boxes in Jewish homes for any other cause but the support of the poor of the Holy Land.

Fifteen years later, Rabbi Jacob David Wilowsky, the Ridvas, famed Talmudic scholar then serving as chief rabbi of Chicago, was asked by the Jewish community of Rochester, New York, whether it would be permissible to use a charity box for the support of a newly established Talmud Torah School, since this additional box might compete with the already present *Meir Ba'al Hanes* box. He replied that it was permitted to do so, even if the poor in Palestine would sustain a loss thereby. His reasoning was that if there were no schools to inculcate the love of Torah and the Holy Land, there would not rise up a generation motivated and trained to support the charity of *Meir Ba'al Hanes*.

Both rabbis were, of course, right, each from his own perspective and experience. For a rabbi in Kovno, living in the midst of a pervasive religious civilization, it was inconceivable that there would ever be a generation of Jews who might not be moved to support their brethren in the Holy Land. The Ridvas, who had come to know the free and open religious cultural atmosphere of America, knew also that the young American Jew had to be inculcated with Jewish sensitivity, trained for Jewish loyalty. The poor of Palestine might sustain a temporary loss through support given to the local school, but in the long run it would be to their benefit that institutions to educate the generations of the future be established and maintained.

Henry Montor himself came to realize that a new and more tranquil relationship had to be established between the UJA and the local communities. He recommended as his successor Dr. Joseph J. Schwartz, the JDC director in Europe, who (in the words of Montor) "had acquired a wonderful reputation." He had supervised relief activities in thirty countries, affecting over one million people, and after the war he had directed the migration to Israel of some five hundred thousand Jews from Europe, Africa, and Asia. Montor's early years were spent as a publicist, and he had an eye for the dramatic and sensational and the capacity to capitalize on them. Schwartz had studied for the rabbinate and had served the Jewish people as a community social worker. His was the ability to understand, to empathize, to work in cooperation rather than confrontation.

The American Jewish community had built its institutions—synagogues, schools, community centers—in the 1920s. The 1930s were the years of the Great Depression, the 1940s years of war, rescue, and rehabilitation. The postwar years had seen the relocation of the Jewish population from the city to the suburbs. New facilities for the established and newly created institutions were high community priorities. Competition for the philanthropic dollar ensued. Schwartz was selfless in his labors for the UJA, but he also recognized that there were legitimate community needs which had a justifiable claim on the communal till. His may also have been the experience and wisdom of the Ridvas, that in the long run the welfare of the UJA and the causes it served would be best secured by a strong and Jewishly committed community. A synagogue, a school, a center may be a competitor to today's campaign, but will also be the surest guarantor of the success of tomorrow's.

The Schwartz years were marked by the consolidation of the UJA into the communal agenda of every community, and by the great and lasting contribution which the UJA made to communal unity and well-being. The relocation into Israel of the Jewries of the Arab countries and their absorption and integration into Israeli society were an enterprise which received the support of all segments of the community and united them in campaign activity; the funds which remained in the community gave the local federations resources with which to establish themselves and assert their hegemony over the community.

As indicated earlier, the appeal of overseas needs had caused a quantum jump in the sums raised by the central Jewish community campaigns. The Schwartz years, 1951–1955, were lean years for the UJA. The needs of the Jews in Moslem lands were not as dramatic as those of the postwar refugees in Europe. Their need to emigrate did not seem quite so urgent. American Jewry, almost wholly of European origin, could identify more with the plight of European Jews. And as was mentioned, American Jewry was turning more to its own communal needs. During the 1951–1955 period, central campaigns averaged some $115 million per year, less than 60 percent of the peak year 1948, but still more than twice as much as the 1945 campaign. The percentage retained by the community went up so that, all in all, the community federations were well recompensed for conducting the campaign. The nonfiscal bonus they received was the addition to the communal lists of contributors and workers whose association heretofore had been minimal, and the sense of community that laboring together in a cause of widest appeal evoked.

The general chairman during these years was Edward M. M. Warburg, son and grandson of the leading communal figures of the previous generations, Felix M. Warburg and Jacob H. Schiff. He had devoted his life to art and communal service, serving since 1941 as chairman of the JDC. By temperament he was most suitable for this era of UJA activity. Contemporaries describe him as "a fine gentleman" with a developed sense of *noblesse oblige*. He was representing American Jewry's premier families, and he did his work with dignity and a sense of duty. His address to the annual national conference of the United Jewish Appeal, on December 12, 1953, reveals his interest and his character:

> The people of Israel have been blessed with the fortune and the privilege of seeing their dream for a land of their own become a reality.
>
> We of the United Jewish Appeal, who began our work at a time of unrelieved darkness and despair, have shared their joy, and the privilege of seeing in our lifetime a measure of restoration made to those of our fellow Jews abroad who suffered but survived. . . . I was recently in Israel—and I came away from Israel with the realization that this is a very grim moment in its history.
>
> But we have faced grim moments before. We came to the present situation as experienced veterans—and we came fortified by the knowledge that we have achieved great things. . . . To the American Jewish community, Israel is vastly important—and we are vastly important to Israel.
>
> If we hold to our vision of long standing—the vision of decency and human dignity for our oppressed fellow Jews—then the people of Israel will hold their frontiers . . . those spiritual frontiers . . . free education, freedom of religion, just courts, the right to vote—the right of men to try to make this world a little better than they found it.

He can't forget... can you?

Note the centrality of Israel in this address by one who was serving and continued to serve for a quarter of a century as chairman of the JDC. Israel had become central to the activities of the UJA and to the life of American Jewry. But it is an American perception of Israel we note, for what is admired most in Israel are just those qualities of freedom, democracy, and sense of mission which have been extolled as the vision and meaning of America. We may note that the UJA thus provides the American Jew with an intimation of his identity and comfortableness in his dual identity as an American and as a Jew, by pointing to the root compatibility of his dual heritage. It suggests to him that his American heritage would indicate support for the UJA and its interest, and the UJA offers him a vehicle for the expression of the mandate of his American heritage "to make this world a little better than [he] found it."

Dr. Schwartz, in his valedictory report in 1955, pointed out that the *national* audience of the UJA may be reckoned at about two million Jews in an economic position to give, and he noted:

From this audience, the UJA year in and year out receives at least the third largest sum made available to any American fund-raising body. . . . Only the U. S. Community Chest movement, with a potential audience of some 50,000,000–60,000,000 able to give, and the American Red Cross, with the same broad audience, raise greater funds than the UJA, and even then—not always. . . . American Jews as a community formed the UJA, gave to it, worked for it, and raised it to the status of an effective, cherished and all-embracing Jewish communal enterprise. . . . The UJA represents a remarkable synthesis of the age-old Jewish recognition of responsibility to one's fellow Jews in need, plus modern American techniques of intensive fund-raising and democratic concepts of social service.

He was able to report that in its first fifteen years the UJA had received over $1 *billion*. With those funds it sustained the one and a half million survivors of the war; it assisted in the emigration of eight hundred eighty-five thousand Jews, 90 percent going to Israel, where it helped in their settlement and economic and social integration; it continued to serve through its constituent agencies the United Israel Appeal, the American Jewish Joint Distribution Committee, and the New York Association for New Americans. In all, it had aided some two and a half million persons, and men and women in 3750 localities in the United States were engaged in its fundraising efforts. His report concluded:

> In Chicago in May 1951, in a UJA meeting which saw American Jews bring forward $15,000,000 in cash, the then Prime Minister of Israel, David Ben-Gurion, summed up the true nature of the UJA effort. . . . Going back to the Greek origin of a much abused word, Mr. Ben-Gurion pointed out that in its original form the word "philanthropy" meant "love of man." He added simply that American Jews by their actions had restored this original meaning—in full.

In 1955, at Ben-Gurion's invitation, Schwartz assumed the professional leadership of the Israel Bond Organization.

15.

At the Tercentenary and Beyond

In 1954, American Jewry celebrated its Tercentenary, the 300th anniversary of the coming to these shores in the summer of 1654 of twenty-three refugees from Recife, South America. This group, consisting of six women, four men, and thirteen children, laid the foundation of what was to become three centuries later the largest, most affluent, and most influential Jewish community in the world. Its more than five and a half million Jews comprised some 45 percent of world Jewry. It had used its political influence to secure its rights at home and to benefit its brethren abroad. In the postwar years it had organized itself and its resources to come to the aid of brethren everywhere.

In the decade which ended in 1954, central Jewish organizations had raised over $1.3 billion. The early campaigns were launched in response to the needs of the Jews orphaned and made homeless in war-blasted Europe. The peak campaign of 1948 celebrated the creation of the State of Israel and pointed to the commitment of American Jewry to help make it a haven for all Jews seeking a home.

By 1951 almost all the displaced persons of Europe had been resettled, some 90 percent in Israel; but 1954 was seeing the intensification of large-scale immigration from North Africa.

After the drama-laden campaign of 1948, there were sharp

annual declines. It was pointed out at that time that "because of the rise in the price level of about 50 percent since 1945, the purchasing power of pledges in 1954 was approximately equal to that of 1945, the last year prior to the post-war emergency period."

In the year of the Tercentenary, American Jewry seemed to be turning more to its domestic needs, and allocations reflected this change. The central campaigns in 1954 showed a decline of 8 percent over 1953, the decline being almost three times that experienced by the 1953 campaign. The percentage allocated for the UJA went from 60 percent in 1953 to 58 percent in 1954. The double decline in amounts raised and allocated decreased the UJA share by almost 10 percent, from $58.2 to $52.5 million. At the same time the allocations to national domestic agencies declined by only 4 percent, and local services received about 2 percent *more* in 1954 than in 1953.

The anomaly was that the local central campaigns, the welfare funds, had grown in quantum leaps because of the appeal of overseas needs. It was the national UJA, as we have seen, which raised the vision and pointed out the philanthropic potential of American Jewry, and provided the motivation for the largest gifts. Often, it was the UJA which found, solicited, and developed the large giver, whose gift was to the local campaign. It thus delivered to community after community generous givers and committed workers who became integrated into the community structure. The popular designation of the local welfare fund campaigns as "UJA Campaigns" pointed to the prevalent perception of their appeal and purpose.

American Jews' most generous response was to the dramatic appeals issued by the UJA. In 1950 they received a copy of the March 14 *Look* magazine article by Ruth Gruber:

AFTER 3000 YEARS

A Bible Prophecy Is Fulfilled

During the generations they suffered in bondage the Jews of Yemen remembered the prophecy of Isaiah. Now, with Ameri-

119

can aid, these 20th century Children of Israel are returning home.

But they that wait upon the Lord shall renew their strength: They shall mount up with wings as eagles. . . .

This was Isaiah's prophecy. Today, nearly 3000 years later, I saw this prophecy fulfilled.

I watched 45,000 modern children of Israel in their flight from bondage in Yemen to freedom in the Promised Land. The first Exodus was led by Moses. The new Children of Israel are led by the United Jewish Appeal in America. The wings are those of an American airlift.

America's Jews read of Operation Magic Carpet and gave to their local welfare fund campaigns for the UJA. Two years later they responded to another challenge:

In 1952, Israel is fighting to preserve the victory of 1948—and to extend it. The enemy is different, but the stakes are just as high. . . . In 1952, Israel's people are again fighting for independence—their economic independence. . . . They fight to turn the great homecoming into the great home-making. In this struggle every American Jew must enlist.

Many, many American Jews read, were moved, responded, enlisted.

A year later American Jewry was challenged by the photograph of a survivor and his wife against a background of Auschwitz, Buchenwald, Dachau, Bergen Belsen . . . clutching a Russian newspaper, captioned:

He can't forget . . . can you?

He hasn't forgotten the nightmare of Nazism. Today's threatening headlines in Pravda won't let him forget.

He thinks, now we must live in fear again—

As long as a strong and growing Israel exists—hope *exists* for those who live in the shadow of fear. Their eyes are turned on that embattled and magnificent young democracy . . . rescuing 750,000 Jews from doom in a few, furiously-paced years. . . . You have helped through the United Jewish Appeal. . . .

The oppressed, the persecuted, the fearful dare to live in hope because of Israel and because of you. Can you deny them that life-sustaining hope? Give generously—*give now.*

Whatever generosity there was in the giving to the 1953 and 1954 campaigns was largely in response to such messages from the United Jewish Appeal. Yet its percentage of the campaign allocation was being cut more drastically than that of others. Some UJA proponents argued that monies raised for overseas needs were being allocated to local and national agencies. If the campaign was, in the popular mind and to the largest contributor, the UJA Campaign, doesn't common honesty demand that allocations be made reflecting that reality? Local community leaders, lay and professional, argued their stance, pointing to the needs at home. In a diminishing campaign picture the confrontation became more pronounced. It was clear to both parties that the partnership which had been established would be maintained, but that the partners would be locked in a continuous struggle for their portions of the income.

To the leadership of the UJA it became obvious that in the years ahead it would need leaders who would not only be able to dramatize the appeal and solicit with imagination and force, but who would also be able to stand up to the local welfare funds in demands and negotiations for UJA's "fair share" of the campaign income. To give such leadership, William Rosenwald was designated national chairman and Herbert A. Friedman was appointed the professional head.

16.

Confrontation and Cooperation

The figure of William Rosenwald stands tall over the forty years of the United Jewish Appeal. He was there at the beginning, and one saw him at sessions of the fortieth annual meeting. From 1942 through 1946 he served as a national cochairman representing the National Refugee Service. From 1955 through 1957 he was general chairman, and in the years before, after, and in between he was an exemplary giver, a diligent worker, and a leader who led by the force of personal example. The great wealth which he inherited and which he acquired, he regarded as a trust to be utilized.

Israel Goldstein viewed him from a Zionist and Jewish communal perspective:

> I must say for Bill Rosenwald that I would list him as number one in the whole category of the non-Zionists from the standpoint of genuine and full-fledged cooperation with the United Jewish Appeal and with the Israel part of it.
>
> Rosenwald was the kind of man who threw himself completely into his work, as if it were his life. . . . I never counted his millions . . . I didn't know his wealth—I don't know whether in proportion to his wealth his gifts were good gifts or whether they were great gifts, extraordinary gifts. But . . . as a leader . . . he

ranks very, very high among his colleagues. . . . He gave more than leadership. He gave intimate, daily, painstaking cooperation. . . . He felt it very, very deeply. This was a very important part of his life. . . . Rosenwald was an outstanding example of UJA leadership and cooperation.

Goldstein stresses "cooperation." The cooperation helped fashion unity in the American Jewish community at its highest levels.

Rosenwald remembers the beginnings of the UJA. While his interests and activities had been with the JDC, as his father's had been, he was a signatory of the agreement which created the UJA. "Actually, I was not particularly sympathetic to Zionism at that time, nor was my father, who, while never anti-Zionist, just thought Zionism impractical. My brother Lessing, on the other hand, was anti-Zionist."

The four decades of activity which followed, most of it for Israel, permitted him to evaluate:

For me it is incredible what we together with other Jews of the diaspora and, of course, the Jews of Israel and the Zionists have been able to accomplish in Israel. To have taken this country and built up all the marvelous things, the industry, the science, the education, the health measures, the agriculture, the strength, is just an incredible achievement.

Above all, I've always been interested in the work from a humanitarian angle primarily. I have found it unbelievable to see the way they've been able to help the people that needed to be rescued from Europe . . . to see the way they absorb them, the Moroccan children. . . . In 1951 we saw little children coming in to Youth Aliyah centers from North Africa. . . . All the children had a frown . . . they looked so inward that I thought they were damaged for life.

But in 1967, when Kfar Rosenwald was dedicated, I saw the same type of young people . . . who had been born in Moslem lands and were fine, fine, handsome, educated, stalwart youth. I never would have believed it possible that you could make people like that out of these North African children.

Only the kind of emotional appeal described by Rosenwald could have elicited the funds and labors he expended. This was no doubt true of many co-workers, in high and low station, who were lured into giving and working by the most rewarding of all promises: to be gifted with the opportunity to save another, to revive him, to restore him to life, to lift him to hope. For those of deeper Jewish national sentiments, the opportunity to participate in the culmination of a national drama of yearning and fulfillment, revival and return, gave meaning and purpose to life. It was an enterprise worthy of the farthest reaches of one's energies and generosity. Once involved, many Jews began to turn inward to the needs of their own commitments.

An anecdote related by the Israeli leader Pinhas Sapir sums up Rosenwald, the UJA worker-leader:

> I worked with Rosenwald several times, and listen, I'm a working man, but I became tired. Early one morning, after I left him (late the night before) I saw him by a public telephone. I asked him, "What are you doing here in the public telephone on Palm Beach?" He said, "I don't want to disturb my wife's rest, so I came to the public telephone where I can talk to some people to solicit them."

Rosenwald rose to the general chairmanship from the inner circles of the UJA. Rabbi Herbert Friedman was brought in from the community. He had a distinguished career as a chaplain in the armed forces immediately after the war. His work with the DP's determined his future. He made his imprint on the community of Denver as a speaker and organizer, was invited to Milwaukee's leading congregation, and was then coopted by the UJA. It was a wise, indeed a fateful decision on the part of Schwartz and Warburg to choose him. Clearly, someone who was intimately acquainted with the American Jewish communal enterprise was now needed, since the UJA had to work with and through the structured community. Declining campaigns and diminished allocations demanded a person from the community to go back to it for cooperation and, if need be, confrontation. The dramatic days of rescue, warfare, and nation founding were now followed by the less exciting labors of settlement and economic and social integration. A creative, vibrant personality was needed to give exciting interpretation to the story. Friedman seemed well suited to the task ahead, and the destiny of this premier American Jewish enterprise was placed in the hands of a thirty-seven-year-old rabbi.

The first and most pressing task was to halt and reverse the erosion of campaign results, which had plummeted by 1954 to but a little more than half the funds raised in 1948—from $205 to $110 million. Friedman, coming from local communal campaign involvement in two typical American Jewish communities, Denver and Milwaukee, knew what national UJA leaders had been claiming: that the potential for giving in the American Jewish community had not yet been adequately addressed, and that only the UJA appeal could tap that reservoir. In 1956 and 1957 a vehicle was created to exploit the latent support for overseas needs. That vehicle was special funds to which one could contribute beyond his usual pledge. In 1956 it was called the UJA Special Survival Fund, and in the next year the UJA Emergency Rescue Fund.

The more than $131 million raised in 1956 was a 20 percent increase and the almost $140 million in 1957 brought the sum to almost a third more in but two years. Overseas needs, in the State of Israel, made for the increases. The incursion of the Soviet Union into the Near East and the Sinai Campaign of 1956 made for heightened concern and lent themselves to dramatic presentation.

The claims of the UJA leadership about potential and appeal were vindicated by these campaigns. "Almost all the increased campaign results for 1956 were channelled to the UJA," the *American Jewish Year Book* reported, and added, "the stimulus of emergency overseas needs was also reflected in a 25 per cent rise in the sale of Bonds for Israel . . . and in $43.6 million in new borrowings by welfare funds for the UJA."

Leaders of the local welfare funds were pleased by the sums realized, but many were not at all happy at the direction of the allocation. For them, local and national needs had equal if not greater priority, and they felt that too little of the money raised was remaining in their cities and in this country. A confrontation between local communities and the UJA ensued.

Herbert Friedman recalled those days:

> Schwartz didn't fight with the communities at all. I lived with the community . . . in a terrible state of tension . . . fighting with them. . . . Relations between the UJA and federation directors . . . were always very, very difficult. . . . The UJA couldn't give any orders . . . but could only persuade them. . . . A huge amount of time was spent . . . trying to convince local federation directors.

Confrontation provided an indirect but nevertheless real benefit to the local communities. It caused the forging of alliances between heretofore contending groups, who laid aside differences to unite for the defense of their communities and for the retention of communal funds for their institutions and organizations. Most communities rose from confrontation with greater unity and strength.

Because the confrontation was with a national body, the UJA, the individual communities felt the need to turn for guidance and support to *their* national body, the Council of Jewish Federations and Welfare Funds. They readily delegated power to the council so that it could face the UJA from a position of strength. The late 1950s and the 1960s were the years when the council began effectively to represent the organized American Jewish community. All recognized the symbiotic relationship between the UJA and the council. The appeal of the UJA brought great sums into the communal coffers; the individual federations and welfare funds provided the machinery and the personnel to raise those funds. As even in the best "marriages," allocation of the available funds can become the source of contention and friction.

In 1950 vigorous attacks were made on the communal fund-raising organizations by some Zionist journalists and organizational leaders. The immediate cause was the criticism by the Institute on Overseas Studies of certain fundraising for Israeli causes conducted by the Council of Jewish Federations and Welfare Funds. It called for greater coordination and efficiency in the expenditure of those funds. The council was accused of attempting to dominate and control Jewish life, and its leadership of being assimilationist, anti-Zionist, anti-democratic, and uninformed and uncommitted Jewishly. When the fervor spent itself and the furor abated, reality took hold. All recognized that practical conditions favored the continued cooperation among Zionists and non-Zionists in the unified fundraising machinery of the UJA nationally and the welfare funds locally. In the years which followed, this basic wisdom continued to operate in American Jewish life.

As we have noted, the local welfare funds delegated their authority and power to the council. In time, delegated power becomes acquired power, and grows beyond that which was received. This was the experience of America, grown from a federal system to an imperial nation. So it was also with the council. The power which it was given, it utilized and developed with great skill and a high degree of responsibility.

The 1960s witnessed the transfer of the central power position in American Jewry from the national organizations to the council. Thus, in the years following the establishment of the State of Israel, Prime Minister Ben-Gurion dealt with Jacob Blaustein, head of the American Jewish Committee, as the representative of effective power in the community, all protestation by the Zionists notwithstanding. Ben-Gurion knew that true power in a voluntary community is in the purse and in the ability to persuade, and correctly perceived where that power lay in the American Jewish community.

In the 1960s, when the need to reconstitute the Jewish Agency became a compelling priority, Louis Pincus, chairman of the executive of the agency, understood that the focus of that power had shifted to the organized large-city communities and that the annual campaigns were the force generating that power. He turned to Max M. Fisher, who had been the general chairman of the United Jewish Appeal and was now president of the Council of Jewish Federations, to join in organizing the new body which came into being in 1971.

Ernest Stock, in his analysis of the reconstituted Jewish Agency, writes: "Where then did the pressure for reconstitution originate on the American side? Behind the UJA in the local communities stood the Jewish federations and welfare funds, and it was there that the mainspring of the drive was to be found."

Herbert Friedman brought with him from his community experiences a number of valuable perceptions about American Jewry. He saw a new community emerging in the postwar world, a community of native-born, highly educated Jews, whose approach to Jewish life was through mind as well as through heart. This community could not be relied on to respond to nostalgia; it had to be presented with knowledge and provided with experiences. The needs of the UJA would have to be taught in the context of the Jewish historic experience, and not merely be dramatized by current emotional appeals. He also concluded that the UJA would be a component of Jewish life for the foreseeable future and that the next generation of leaders would have to be prepared, a group for whom philanthropy would grow out of a more wide-reaching Jewish commitment, whose assumption of responsibility would be in response to their studied conception of Jewish duty. A cadre of such leaders would assume positions of leadership in their respective communities. They would become a force in fundraising, and would constitute a corps of influential UJA loyalists in their local federations.

Friedman is correct in his assessment that "the Young Leadership Cabinet is one of the most important things which the UJA developed." Philip Bernstein, executive vice-president of the Council of Jewish Federatons since 1955, concurs:

Herb Friedman . . . felt that he would like to involve a number of young people directly in UJA as a young leadership cabinet. He reached out to involve them in Israel and Europe and in fund raising responsibility. He got them involved in the UJA to deepen their commitment, and then had them go back to their communities to serve their own Federations. So, the UJA has been a force there [young leadership development], a very important force in recent years.

Friedman went on to describe the concept, its organization, and its launching:

I was convinced in my own mind that we had to try to find a new generation of leaders and that we had to train them and motivate them. For a year . . . from the fall of 1959 through the spring of 1960 . . . I went around to every meeting of the UJA . . . looking for young men who stood out above the crowd, either by the way they spoke or by the way they gave money or by the way other people followed them. I had 300–400 names by the time I finished . . . then decided to call a conference . . . [in] September 1960. In the spring I wrote to the executive directors in the communities telling them what I was going to do. . . . It was absolutely remarkable how they all said, "No, don't do it, it is not your job." . . . In November . . . I called a meeting and 250 people came . . . all at their own expense. . . . Nobody believed there would be such a number and such quality. . . . I decided what I would try to give them would be an educational lecture . . . of four hours, or six hours . . . the subject: one hundred years of Jewish history . . . 1880 to 1980 (the last twenty years were a projection). . . . I gave them a history lesson. . . . I tried to make them proud of being Jews and being connected to Israel. And then at the end, I left them with the feeling that they had a big responsibility. . . . I said, "If you want to take part in this, you have to enlist as a soldier for the rest of your life."

Many who attended the opening conference look back on it as a transforming experience in their lives. They remember the lecture and its challenge. They recall receiving and reading books, attending study sessions, and returning to their communities demanding work and assuming leadership. Some complained that the old were reluctant to make room for the young in positions of leadership, and that there were among them those who fell by the wayside when the excitement wore off, or when they found that apprenticeship and exemplary giving were demanded as the price of leadership. But there were many who remained to labor, to give, to lead, and to lift their lives to new plateaus of significance and satisfaction.

One hundred young men and women from forty-two communities participated in the first UJA Young Leadership Mission to Europe and Israel, among them Irwin S. Field who seventeen years later became general chairman of the United Jewish Appeal. The Israel experience became central in the fundraising effort. Prospects came, saw, were solicited in the "back of the bus," and returned home to work in the local campaign.

The late 1950s and early 1960s were lean years. The 1957 level of giving was not reached again for a decade. But one gets the feeling that these years would have been leaner yet had it not been for the hard-driving and demanding campaigns launched by the UJA. Those were difficult times for campaigns based on overseas needs, for history did not provide any dramatic events overseas. Now long-delayed, needed projects at home competed for the philanthropic dollar.

Among these projects were new synagogue buildings in the suburbs of the urban centers where Jews were settling in increasing numbers in the postwar years. In a climate of universal respect for established religions, the American Jew opted for a communal identity as a "religious community." Judaism became a counterpart of Protestantism and Catholicism, and it was not lost on the American Jew that the posture of a religious community in "The Land of the Three Great Faiths" lifted American Jewry from the designation as one of many ethnic groups to the status of one-third of America. For reasons theological and sociological, Jews in large numbers were affiliating with congregations, and rabbis were taking their place with ministers and priests as respected and influential members of the community.

Relations between congregations and federations were strained. Differences in the priorities of Jewish endeavors and competition for funds made for tension in many communities. Rabbis and federation executives were often at odds for reasons ideological and practical.

Friedman, who had experienced communal and congregational life firsthand as an influential rabbi, moved to strengthen the UJA through utilization of the above-mentioned realities in American Jewish life. Why not place rabbi and congregation in service of the cause? Certainly it was a cause dear to both, one to which both could contribute. He thereupon launched the national UJA Rabbinical Advisory Cabinet (currently, the Rabbinic Cabinet).

A cornerstone of this cabinet's operation was the "100 Percent Plan." Each rabbi was asked to review the membership list of his congregation against the federation gift list. Each congregation was to strive for a 100 percent record of giving by all members of the synagogue. The synagogue was to become involved in the fundraising effort of the federation. The rabbi was to have a central role in the enterprise. Such an endeavor would raise congregation and federation out of their mutual suspicion and recrimination and bring them together in cooperative enterprise. The rabbi had the opportunity for a meaningful and respected role in communal affairs, for he could now demonstrate that he was ready to undertake that which he was preaching. To organize the rabbinic effort, a national UJA Rabbinic Cabinet was formed, chaired successively by Orthodox, Conservative, and Reform rabbis.

The 100 Percent Plan achieved 100 percent success in only a limited number of congregations, but it did add thousands of names to federation rosters. It established between congregation and federation a new type of relationship which contributed to communal cooperation and unity. It brought many rabbis into communal activities, to the benefit of both. The

Well done, but . . .
NOT ALL DONE

Each week the atmosphere surrounding the port of Haifa becomes charged with emotion. The SS Transylvania steams into the harbor from Rumania carrying upwards of 2,000 men, women and children. A new—and hopeful—life begins for the newcomers as they set foot on Israel's soil. At Lydda airport, in central Israel, the same scenes of joy enacted at Haifa are repeated as planes wing in from Teheran with Jews saved from Iran's fearful political climate.

The American Jewish community, through the United Jewish Appeal, has been making possible the transfer to Israel of tens of thousands of homeless Jews every year since the end of World War II. This historic task of rescue has been carried out in the face of persistent crises and emergencies. Israel—with United Jewish Appeal aid—has received more than 750,000 Jewish men, women and children since V-E Day.

It has been a job well done—but it is not all done.

Emigration deadlines loom for hundreds of thousands of homeless Jews who must be transferred to Israel from Eastern Europe and the Moslem world, 60,000 of them before December 31. Desperately-needed temporary homes must be constructed for 150,000 recent newcomers to Israel. More than 400,000 destitute Jews in Europe, North Africa and the Near East must be furnished with vital food and medical supplies, while 10,000 Jewish immigrants due in the United States this fall must be given a helping hand.

Through the UJA, you helped rescue the homeless and resettle the uprooted. Your support of the campaign in your community made it possible for the United Jewish Appeal record miraculous feats of rescue and rehabilitation.

Now—before it's too late—you must help finish the historic task that began when World War II ended.

The United Jewish Appeal and its agencies—the United Palestine Appeal, Joint Distribution Committee and United Service for New Americans—must have your support, in pledges and in cash.

Let's get the whole job done before we say it's been well done! Let's see the job through—now!

annual rabbinic missions to Israel afforded one of the few opportunities for rabbis of the three religious groups to live and labor together. Nor should it go unnoticed that the UJA strengthened its position with rabbis and congregational leaders, for it offered them opportunities for significant communal labors, which many federations had denied them.

Friedman was responsible for a creative tension which confrontations between the UJA and the federations brought to Jewish life. The special funds reversed the downward trend of the campaigns; the Young Leadership Cabinet has continued to provide new leadership to the UJA and the individual federations; the Rabbinic Cabinet has encouraged greater unity in the American rabbinate, and has brought rabbis into useful communal service and leadership; and the network of UJA missions has placed Israel in a position of centrality not only in the campaign but in the life of vast numbers of American Jews as well. All have set examples to other organizations of imaginative exploitation of opportunities available and have taught how these are to be organized, launched, and administered.

UJA overseas missions in particular have had a galvanizing effect on the level of both fundraising and commitment in the Jewish communities of America. Prior to the Six-Day War, UJA-organized visits to Israel were selectively limited to the foremost leaders and contributors, or to constituency groups assembled by the national Women's Division and Young Leadership Cabinet. The pride and euphoria resulting from the Six-Day War generated a deep desire among communities to see and share in the growth and dynamism of the triumphant Jewish state.

Community professionals and the national UJA staff and leadership instantly understood that the mission experience was ideally suited to channeling that impulse into directions favorable to strengthening both campaign and community. As developed by national UJA expertise and experience, the missions program exposed participants effectively to the accomplishments of Israel's people through itineraries encompassing meetings with the country's foremost leaders and a wide-ranging survey of the human-support programs of the Jewish Agency. This created a uniquely effective environment for the solicitation of maximum campaign gifts from the participants, and sent them back to their communities as more knowledge-able and qualified solicitors. Missions thus became both a sym-bol and an expression of the national unity of fundraising purpose and action between the Israel-oriented UJA campaign and the federated communities which annually carried it out.

From the handfuls and hundreds who went on UJA missions in the 1950s and 1960s, primarily as individuals and divisional constituents, the number of participants in the 1970s grew into the tens of thousands, mainly consisting of compact community units. The percentage of pledge increases achieved has con-sistently surpassed the average national increase. UJA missions, which have included variant or additional visits to points of historic and contemporary Jewish interest in Europe and North Africa, have been voyages of discovery for the growing number of participants, revealing the use of community-raised funds for what has been called the "lifeline" work overseas of the JDC and the Jewish Agency.

17.

Leadership from the Community

Henry Morgenthau, Jr., came to the UJA leadership from the highest office ever held by a Jew in America, secretary of the treasury. His successor as UJA general chairman, Edward M. M. Warburg, put on the mantle of leadership worn before him by his distinguished father and before that by his even more distinguished grandfather. William Rosenwald continued the exemplary giving initiated by his father, whose philanthropy had set new standards in the Jewish community. They all invested the office with family prestige and dignity to which they added their own measure of devotion and hard work. They also represented an era in American Jewish life which was coming to an end. For over one hundred years leadership in the Jewish community had been the prerogative of Jews who came from the German states, or their children and grandchildren. Morgenthau, Warburg, and Rosenwald were the last national leaders to be thought of as members of that elite.

The postwar years witnessed the ascendancy of the sons and daughters of the eastern European immigrant community into positions of leadership in their local communities and on the national scene. The "old guard" leadership was provided by history; the new leadership was "geographic," coming to the national scene from service and leadership in their local communities. The new leadership was thus the product of a process of "natural democracy" which rewards merit with the palm of office. To the credit of the leaders who had accepted the gift of leadership which history had proffered them, they permitted and encouraged "natural democracy" to take its course, and remained on to aid their successors.

The first of the new leaders, Morris W. Berinstein, from Syracuse, New York, depended heavily on the advice and guidance of prior major leaders who remained prominently active in the campaign. As a veteran UJA leader remembers, Berinstein was "running it [the UJA] with Eddie Warburg and Bill Rosenwald. . . . That was about the extent of it." The Midwest provided Berinstein's successor, Philip M. Klutznick. Born in Kansas City, raised in Omaha, later making his home in Chicago, he had served as international president of B'nai B'rith and in a number of important governmental positions. His expertise in planning new communities was utilized in the development of the Israeli seaport, Ashdod. Klutznick's tenure as general chairman was cut short by a presidential appointment to serve as ambassador to the United Nations Economic and Social Council.

Joseph Meyerhoff, who took office in 1961, had come with his family from Russia in 1906. Morgenthau's father, Henry Sr., had been a doctrinaire anti-Zionist; Julius Rosenwald was a practical anti-Zionist; Felix Warburg and Jacob H. Schiff had been non-Zionists; but Meyerhoff's father was a Zionist. His son recalls:

As a matter of fact, in the early nineteen hundreds he went to Palestine from Russia to see if he should move his family there. . . . He lived there for several months, and came away convinced that it was too rough a place to raise a family. So he went back to Russia. My father was head of the local defense group (against pogroms) in the small town near Poltava where we lived. They came searching for arms in the middle of the night . . . put my father in political prison for two months. . . . In 1906, when my father was able to get a passport, we all came to the United States to Baltimore.

The plight of Jews was an experience with which Meyerhoff's generation could identify. Indeed, they or members of their immediate family had experienced persecution and homelessness, followed by new life and new hope. This gave their leadership in Jewish causes, in the UJA, an immediacy and urgency which generated a high degree of effectiveness. Meyerhoff's story is that of many of his generation:

> When I went into business I became as active and involved as I could in Jewish causes. I worked with charities and in the early UJA campaigns. . . . By the early forties I was one of the vice-chairmen in the campaign here [in Baltimore]. . . . In 1949 they asked me to be the local UJA chairman. . . . At that time, the Welfare Fund and the Associated Jewish Charities were separate groups. We alternated campaigns between them . . . we would ask for two-year pledges, later . . . one-year pledges. . . . The Associated didn't campaign for about three years because of the priorities of 1946, 1947, 1948. During 1949 and 1950 we had our first joint campaign.

Like many other communities, Baltimore had its separate local and overseas campaigns. Most often the older German Jewish community was identified with the former and the more recent eastern European group with the latter. The two campaigns not only reflected the divided community but also made for a prolongation of that division. The joint campaign which overseas needs forced on the community did much to unite it not only for fundraising but for all manner of communal endeavor and social intercourse as well. The last such division, that in New York City, was erased by the Yom Kippur War.

Local UJA leadership led to national involvement. A UJA mission to Israel in 1949 evoked memories:

> Two hundred and fifty thousand people were living in tents . . . they baked in the summer and froze in the winter. . . . At Haifa,

where they first came in . . . they set up little schools. . . . I went to a couple of classes. I remember it reminded me of the first time I came to Baltimore. . . . We had a class at the German-English school where I went, and its memory was most vivid for me when I saw those kids in Sha-ar Aliyah learning.

Memory made for the mandate: "In 1949, I said that I wanted to devote the next ten best years of my life, as I figured they would be, to helping develop the economy of the country." A little more than a decade later, Meyerhoff became general chairman of the UJA. The chairmanship made demands on time, resources, and energies of the incumbent. His gift had to set an example, but that was perhaps the easiest. Each year had its mission to Israel and with it the nagging frustration that no matter how successful the campaign, it would not nearly answer even the most immediate needs. And campaigns those years were difficult. Communities were resisting the special funds which had been designed to halt the erosion of income. Communities had to be visited, their leaderships confronted and won over. Meyerhoff reports:

> Los Angeles didn't want to have a Special Fund. . . . We finally convinced them saying, "If we can go out and get eight or ten contributions of twenty-five to fifty thousand dollars each, will you let us have the Special Fund, provided none of last year's gifts were cut? . . . We wouldn't take a gift from anyone if they didn't agree to continue their gift for this year at last year's amount." . . . I said, "I guarantee you'll raise the amount from last year so you have nothing to lose." This is the way we finally sold the Special Fund to them. We actually got half a dozen contributions of twenty-five to fifty thousand and more. Each one was solicited personally. We had to argue with the boards of the communities. . . . This is the kind of work we did constantly. . . . The battles in those days were unbelievable.

As is so often the case, the vanquished became the chief beneficiaries. The UJA forced the special fund on the communities and it personally solicited the pace-setting gifts for it.

Eventually these special fund monies became integrated into the general welfare fund campaign, with all the benefits which accrued to the local communities from larger campaign incomes. No matter what way a campaign is designated or how it is organized, the power of making allocations from the *total* funds raised by the central communal agency is vested in that agency, the federation of the local community. When a special fund is launched, the regular fund continues its activity. When allocations are made from the special fund, it is reasonable to assume that the federation allocations committees and boards will not be unaware of or unaffected in their decisions by the sums raised by special funds. Meyerhoff recalls:

> The Council of Federations, during the three or four years I was UJA Chairman, was trying to become the dominant force in fund raising in the United States. They tried to put the UJA in the same category as every other beneficiary of the Welfare Funds. Of course, I fought the attempt tooth and nail. We finally compromised the matter in my last year as Chairman, or perhaps a year after, when Max Fisher came into the picture.

Max M. Fisher came to national leadership through activity in the Detroit Jewish community. He had served as president of its Jewish Welfare Federation, one of the most powerful in the nation. A leading industrialist, he had also risen to a position of influence in the Republican party, serving on its national committee. To his office as general chairman he brought the power attendant upon a successful business career, the experience of Jewish communal leadership, and the aura of political influence. He went on to become president of the Council of Jewish Federations and Welfare Funds, while serving at the same time as chairman of the United Israel Appeal; he later became chairman of the Board of Governors of the reconstituted Jewish Agency, as well as chairman of the executive committee of the American Jewish Committee. He thus had positions of leadership in all the power bases of the American Jewish community. In a sense, he also represented the final consolidation of the Jewish community into a united, unified entity. It is significant to note that his first position of national leadership was in the UJA. It was the one enterprise which could serve as both coalescing agent and the fountainhead of united Jewish communal enterprise.

In 1966, in his second year as general chairman, Fisher received the American Judaism Award of the Reform Jewish Appeal. In his response he spoke of the inner meaning of "giving":

> *Fortune* magazine reported that the Jewish "gross national product" for philanthropic purposes runs to something over 625 million dollars a year, a generous outpouring which it characterized as "The miracle of Jewish giving." *Newsweek* magazine was less kind. Most of the people it quoted had sharp things to say about the intensity of Jewish fundraising, and it reported at least one scholar as decrying all such activity as a kind of "checkbook" Judaism. . . . To me . . . it is a matter of greatest pride that in the 20 years since the end of World War II, American Jews through Welfare Funds and the United Jewish Appeal have raised two-and-one-half billion dollars to strengthen Jewish community life at home, to save Jews overseas, to reconstruct Jewish life abroad, to build Israel, and to rescue 1,750,000 survivors and bring them to Israel and other free lands. . . .
>
> How then can anyone, looking at this great giving for survival, so misread it as to call it "checkbook" Judaism?

To Fisher, and to other Jews of similar background, the welfare funds and the United Jewish Appeal were but two sides of the coin of the American Jewish philanthropic enterprise. It is the coin of the realm in American Jewish life. For most American Jews in the 1960s, philanthropy, specifically for overseas needs, was the first and most common denominator of identification with the Jewish people, and the United Jewish Appeal welfare funds were the vehicle and symbol of this most basic American Jewish activity. Fisher, whose training for national leadership had taken place in a tightly organized and highly disciplined Jewish community, early recognized the symbiotic relationship between the UJA and the welfare fund locally, and the UJA—Council of Jewish Federations and Welfare Funds nationally. His own stature as a leader assured close cooperation between the two during his leadership of both. In the summer of 1967, the cooperation which had been established served American Jewry and the State of Israel well in a moment of unprecedented crisis.

18.

The Summer of 1967 and the Fall of 1973

The Six-Day War in June 1967 had the profoundest of effects on American Jewry. An intensified Jewish consciousness, a sense of the oneness of Jewish destiny, a heightened commitment to the priority of Jewish interests and welfare, and an outpouring of unprecedented generosity engulfed community after community. It was immediately visible in a newfound will and ability to give which expressed itself through the central Jewish community campaigns. Campaign figures tell the story:

YEAR	APPEAL		MONEY RAISED (MILLIONS)
1965			$131.3
1966			$136.5
1967	Regular	$144.5	
	Emergency	$173.0	$317.5
1968	Regular	$152.6	
	Emergency	$ 80.0	$232.6
1969	Regular	$162.9	
	Emergency	$ 99.0	$261.9
1970	Regular	$174.2	
	Emergency	$124.0	$298.2

What is most noteworthy is that the regular campaign total continued to increase and the "Emergency campaign" became a regular, accepted feature of the annual campaign. (It should also be noted that in the three years of 1967–1969, $428,687,000 in State of Israel Bonds were sold in the United States, more than a third of the total sales of the previous nineteen years.) The accomplishments in the last half of the decade of the Israel Education Fund, launched by UJA in 1964 to aid secondary education in Israel, are also significant. Although the IEF, which accepted gifts of $100,000 and more above the regular UJA commitment, yielded to the primacy of the emergency fund in the immediate postwar years, it was still able to report pledges of $30 million by the end of the five-year period.

By 1971, the record giving of 1967 was surpassed, rising to $375 million in 1972 and $380 million in 1973. The monies realized in these community campaigns were allocated not only for overseas relief but for national and local institutions and organizations as well. As a historian of the period wrote:

> The appeal was to the American Jews' interest in resettlement and rehabilitation abroad, and the bulk of the money was channeled to the United Jewish Appeal, but the Jewish defense agencies, Jewish education, Jewish health services, and cultural enterprises at home benefited from this joint philanthropic endeavor. The campaign process, with its program of educational rallies and meetings addressed by leaders of Israel and American Jewry, and with its missions to Israel, served as a bridge and a bond between the communities of Israel and America.

Accounts of spontaneous and enthusiastic giving in the summer of 1967 have become part of American Jewish folklore. At a luncheon in New York, one man pledged $1.55 million, and four others $1 million each. It is said that $15 million was pledged in fifteen minutes. Fifty families in Boston contributed $2.5 million to launch the drive. In Cleveland $3 million was raised in a day, and over a million in St. Louis overnight. Throughout the country children went into the streets with pails, milk bottles, and cans to collect for the emergency. On campuses, students went from door to door in their dormitory buildings. *Yeshiva* students spread through the Times Square and garment districts of New York, taking contributions in bedsheets.

The more than half a billion dollars which the campaign and bond sales produced was the result of more than spontaneous giving, no matter how fervent. It demanded planning, organization, execution, and a united Jewry to undertake and accomplish it.

Philip Bernstein, executive vice-president of the Council of Jewish Federations, recalls:

> When the war broke out in 1967 . . . I called one community after another, one federation after another . . . to urge that they mobilize the utmost cash immediately. . . . The UJA and we . . . had a joint mobilization, Herbert Friedman who was the executive . . . and lay heads Eddie Ginsberg, Max Fisher . . . who were in leadership at that time. . . . We met with the UJA literally every day to work together. . . . The UJA concentrated on big gifts. I sat in the office of Herb Friedman when he was calling people who had given a hundred thousand to ask for a million or two million. . . . It was all worked out with the communities. . . . Then in a historic luncheon, when the mobilization was completed, they took a picture of the people, twenty or thirty people. It was a joint group as you can see.

A delegation of the Council of Jewish Federations and Welfare Funds which visited Israel in September 1967 was able to report: "We found . . . a new recognition of the extraordinary work our federations and welfare funds had accomplished for the Israel Emergency fund . . . and, even more fundamentally, a new understanding of the continuing central role of our community organizations in American and worldwide Jewish life."

One may add that it was the recognition by the leaders of the federations of the centrality of Israel in the communal campaign efforts that was so crucial to the establishment of that central role. This recognition also led to a desire on the part of the American Jewish establishment leadership to be more fully involved in the drama of a nation reborn and rebuilding. It took practical expression in the reconstitution of the Jewish Agency in 1971, which the council hailed: "The historic first assembly of the Reconstituted Jewish Agency for Israel which met in Jerusalem June 21–25 marked a turning point in the cooperation of Jewish communities throughout the world with each other and with the people of Israel."

Max M. Fisher, the leading figure of the council and the United Jewish Appeal, spoke the prevailing sentiment of American Jewry in its relationship to Israel at the final session of the first assembly:

> Out of this land once came a great message to the world: justice, freedom and human dignity. And we Jews, we choose to believe that out of this land will yet come another such message. To be given a chance to make our contribution to that goal, to be able to do our part by re-establishing our people, to build for peace that will surely come, to have a small share in creating that Israel. . . . All this is a privilege beyond price.

The UJA had brought the council to the recognition of the central role of Israel—nation and state reborn—in the consciousness and life of the American Jew, and had brought the American Jew to that consciousness. The deed fashions the attitude. Long and generous participation in the enterprise of aiding by sharing created the sentiment that it is "a privilege beyond price."

The post-1967 UJA efforts were carried on with a manic zeal in a community in which giving grew beyond duty to privilege. The energy and creativity of Herbert Friedman were matched by the general chairman, Edward Ginsberg, an articulate spokesman, a tireless campaigner, and an exceedingly effective solicitor. It was this team that was responsible for the reversal of the expected postwar decline by 1971.

Ginsberg, an attorney, came to national UJA leadership from a career of service to the Jewish community of Cleveland, perhaps the best organized American Jewish community. He had served it as general chairman of the Jewish Community Federation in 1960–1961, and as president of his congregation, the Fairmount Temple. In the fateful days of 1967 he led a four-member UJA team to Israel, and took leadership of the campaign thereafter. His community service was directed by a view of Jewish life which emphasized community and faith, community expressed in the oneness of the Jewish people in history and geography, and a faith which is comprised of equal measures of stubbornness, determination, and duty. His address at the UJA National Conference, on December 13, 1969, gives expression to these views:

> They have been trying to erase us from the face of this earth for two thousand years. . . . We have a tough fibre, a moral fibre that just won't erase. . . .
> Now more than ever it is a time to stand indivisible. . . . We must not fear because we are servants of the Lord and we will not be fainthearted. . . .
> The Israelis won't be fainthearted. . . . Let us give them the tools . . . to be educated . . . to house . . . to heal . . . to bring 60,000 people this year. . . . We are going to have a campaign with the biggest and broadest scope in the history of philanthropy. . . . By our giving and by our solidarity, that is how we give them the tools.

A co-worker sums up the man and his singular contribution: "Edward Ginsberg was the man who travelled around the country more than anyone else and was the best solicitor of major giving that the UJA had in terms of its volunteer leadership. . . . He brought to fund raising new dimensions of voluntarism and leadership."

The changes in the psyche of the American Jew, his redefinition of his Jewishness and reordering of his priorities wrought by the Six-Day War, were nowhere more evident than in the new and unexpected phenomenon of a significant number of American Jews talking of and undertaking *aliyah*. In the years 1967–1970, more American Jews settled in Israel than in the previous twenty years. Many had first experienced Israel in UJA missions, or in the growth of tourism. Among those making the decision "to go on *Aliyah*" was Herbert Friedman. The long, creative, and highly effective professional UJA leadership of Friedman came to an end.

The UJA chose as his successor Irving Bernstein, who had spent almost his entire professional life in the service of the UJA. He was the consummate professional, who had mastered the campaign apparatus and was skilled in its utilization. The campaigns of 1972 and 1973, which he directed professionally under the chairmanship of Paul Zuckerman, exceeded the record year of 1967, indicating that the proper choice had been made.

There is no general agreement among students of American Jewish communal life about which is the best organized Jewish community in America, but most would agree that it is either Cleveland or Detroit. It was fitting then that Detroit's Paul Zuckerman should follow Cleveland's Edward Ginsberg as general chairman in 1972. A man of energy, heart, and determination, his career of Jewish service is as wide as Jewish philanthropy, with a special emphasis on education. His was the task of directing into effective and constructive channels the vast energies and unprecedented capacity for generosity generated in the American Jewish community by the Yom Kippur War. On June 27, 1973, he announced: (1) a meeting at the home of Ambassador Simcha Dinitz on August 20, limited to thirty-six persons, each from a major city "prepared to make a pacesetting gift"; (2) a prime minister's mission on August 27–31, to Israel, comprised of the local chairman and two major givers of cities raising a million dollars or more; (3) a national study conference for donors of $20,000 and over on October 21–30, "preceded by four sub-missions to Iran, Denmark, Poland, Austria, Yugoslavia, and Poland."

UJA was a global operation, providing American Jewish leaders the opportunity to visit and associate with fellow Jews in many lands. But Israel remained central in its concerns and

activities, and in its appreciation. Zuckerman expressed this at
the UJA's annual meeting in December of 1973:

> We are truly unique. It is the pattern of history that countries at
> war are filled with refugees who are only too eager to *leave* the
> country. Jews, especially Soviet Jews, coming as they did *during*
> the war, demonstrated not only the spirit of Jewish survival but
> the necessity for an Israel. The gates never closed, not even for an
> instant.

It was during Zuckerman's incumbency that the UJA began to
surpass the 1967 level of giving.

The years 1971–1972 saw the beginning of large-scale immigration to Israel from the Soviet Union. This new wave,
which was as dramatic as it was unexpected, brought thirteen
thousand Jews in 1971 and thirty-five thousand in 1972. For
more than half a century, the second-largest Jewish community
in the world had been cut off from world Jewry. The gates had
first opened in 1966–1970, permitting a slow trickle to Israel, a
little more than five thousand emigrants. Now the possibility
that the trickle might become a wave moved world Jewry to
action.

American Jewry took the leadership in pressing the U.S.
government to use its influence on its fellow superpower. It also
assumed responsibility for the relocation and resettlement of
those permitted to leave. History had handed the UJA a new
mandate, and America's Jewry was ready to respond. The UJA
was ready; organized Jewry gave its fullest cooperation, the
machinery of rescue and rehabilitation was reactivated, and a
new chapter in the rebirth of the Jewish people in the post-
Holocaust era was being written.

When the Arab armies from the west and from the north
attacked at 2 P.M. on October 6, 1973, the Jews of the East
Coast of America were on their way to their synagogues for the
Yom Kippur service. In the Midwest it was 7:00 A.M., and on
the West Coast 5:00 A.M. It was from the pulpits that

America's Jews first heard the news. Prayer took on a new significance and urgency. There was an urgency, too, for the Holy Day to come to an end, so that the practical work might begin which this new and apparently greatest emergency demanded.

In 1967 it was the war which brought together for joint effort the professional and lay leaderships of both the UJA and the council. In 1973 it was most natural for Irving Bernstein to call Philip Bernstein, and for them and their lay leaders to meet in the home of Zev Sher, the Israeli economic minister stationed in New York, immediately after breaking the fast. A mobilization of the American Jewish community was launched on Sunday at a meeting attended by some seventy-five leaders of the UJA and the council. Israel's finance minister Pinhas Sapir requested that $100 million in cash be gathered within the week.

Daniel J. Elazar, in his study "The American Jewish Response to the Yom Kippur War," reports:

> The response was everything anyone expected and more. The $107 million raised was accompanied by stories of men borrowing money at high interest rates to provide cash, people mortgaging their houses, women giving jewels. . . . Congregations called special meetings to pray for Israel's victory and to raise funds to make that victory possible. . . . On Tuesday night, October 9, communities across the country held open rallies to raise funds . . . sound trucks were driven through the streets of Jewish neighborhoods and suburbs asking for contributions. Hats and coin boxes were passed at rallies. . . . Student gifts for the UJA far exceeded any previous campus effort, with $700,000 reported the first month alone. . . . There were three gifts of $5 million, several of $2 million or more and some forty gifts of $1 million or more. . . .
>
> As a general rule, the better organized the campus, the greater the amount of money that was raised. The same held true for faculty giving. . . .
>
> The major funds came from the relatively small number of very big donors and generally from those who had already been

identified as big contributors. . . . Relatively few new people came forward. . . .

If the fund-raising drive had any major weakness, it was the failure to reach down properly to middle-level and small givers. . . . The biggest givers . . . have been well educated regarding Israel's needs . . . middle range givers have not yet been subjected to the same kind of educational efforts.

One can draw from this analysis an appreciation for the success of the UJA's efforts to cultivate the "big donors," and a challenge to the community federations to do better with their constituency of middle-range and smaller givers.

As an astute political scientist Elazar places great emphasis on "The Advantages of Organization":

Improvements in the organizational framework introduced since 1967 made a great difference. . . . Two important factors stand out in connection with the fund-raising responses: the effect of education and the effect of organization on the overall effort.

The best response came from people who had been educated to appreciate Israel's situation and needs . . . through various young leadership programs . . . who had been to Israel to get an intensive view of the situation, who had been educated through seminars and conferences in the United States and whose general consciousness had been raised by these efforts of the federation movements and the UJA. . . .

The educational achievement would not have come about without the availability of the organizational framework to stimulate and manage it. . . . The Yom Kippur War offers a classic case of how organization makes the whole greater than the sum of its parts.

The anxious days in 1967 were the days in May which preceded the outbreak of hostilities. In 1973 the time of worry was during the war's duration and after. In 1967 the outpouring of generosity was in a mood of concern turned to one of celebration and gratitude. In 1973 the giving was in an atmosphere of impending peril. The more serious and more dedicated Jew felt that all was at stake, and that the situation demanded sacrificial response. After the cessation of hostilities, most American Jews recognized that increased giving which the crisis evoked would have to continue in large measure, to aid a people in Israel who would have to devote so large a portion of its GNP to security needs.

The $660 million raised in the campaign of 1974 was almost $200 million more than in the previous year. Much of the campaign's success may be attributed to what Elazar termed "education," an education which makes for a conditioned response in a crisis situation. That the campaigns which followed the war crisis could raise almost $100 million more than the last precrisis year may be credited to "the educational achievement" plus "the organizational framework."

The fundraising apparatus of the UJA was in the hands of trained, tested, and devoted lay leaders, and a corps of skilled and devoted veteran professionals. It was augmented by increased personnel in many local federations.

Education was promoted and expanded by the national UJA. Irving Bernstein was the first of the UJA chief executives who had not had rabbinic training. Perhaps that is why he recognized even more than his predecessors the UJA need and responsibility to make its contribution to intensify Jewish identity and raise Jewish consciousness.

The international conference on the Holocaust, which the UJA cosponsored with the Hebrew University in New York in March 1975, was a chief influence in placing the Holocaust on the academic agenda of American scholarship, and introducing its study on many American university campuses.

In his history of American Zionism We Are One, Melvin Urofsky writes, "Irving Bernstein, executive vice-president of the UJA, believes that before the 1967 war, the campaign was used to raise funds; now it is used to raise Jews."

Rabbi Leo Baeck has called attention to an operational paradox which has given a unique and distinctive vitality to Judaism: that which is of God must yet become so through man.

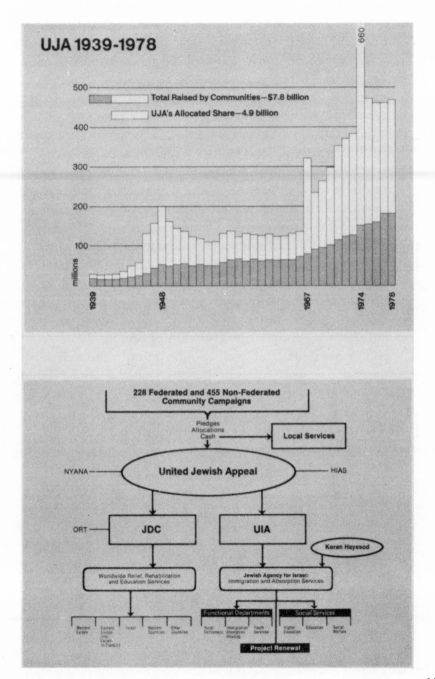

UJA 1939-1978

Total Raised by Communities—$7.8 billion

UJA's Allocated Share—4.9 billion

228 Federated and 455 Non-Federated Community Campaigns

Pledges
Allocations
Cash

Local Services

NYANA — United Jewish Appeal — HIAS

ORT — JDC   UIA

Keren Hayesod

Worldwide Relief, Rehabilitation and Education Services

Jewish Agency for Israel: Immigration and Absorption Services

Functional Departments   Social Services

Project Renewal

One born a Jew must still *become* a Jew through will and act, through expression of responsibility and assumption of duty. No mere accident of birth or arrival at a point in time will do. A friend and co-worker said of Frank R. Lautenberg, "He became a Jew in '67." Ginsberg and Zuckerman had been prepared by community activity to serve their people in an hour of crisis; it was the challenge of a crisis facing his people that brought Lautenberg to Jewish service and leadership.

A successful scientist-industrialist, he brought his training and skills to the UJA leadership, and with it a deep and growing appreciation for the uniqueness of the Jewish heritage and the oneness of the Jewish people. On his reelection as UJA general chairman in 1975, he called upon fellow Jews "to bear witness, in a world unconcerned with decency and common respect for humanity, to the eternity of the Jewish people. . . . For wherever Jewish people inhabit this earth, we are bound together by remembering, by tradition, by faith, by our refusal to succumb to indifference . . . by our affirmation of life."

That statement followed by one month the infamous "Zionism is racism" resolution at the United Nations. From that moment on, the energies of the UJA national leadership, guided by the Lautenberg-Bernstein team, were directed toward the planning and implementation of a historic declaration of unity with Israel's people which was, in effect, a super-mission. The event, called "This Year in Jerusalem," sent a flotilla of jets into Israel in the fall of 1976, carrying three thousand Jewish men and women from hundreds of communities of all sizes in all fifty states into every corner of Israel in a demonstration of solidarity which visibly moved and heartened even the most skeptical of Israelis.

More than ever before, "This Year in Jerusalem" underlined the power of Israel in the life of American Jewish communities, exposed the emotional heart of their essentially Israel-oriented campaigns, and highlighted the UJA's role as a catalyst in providing the means for effective community expression of oneness with Israel's people. It was one of the most dramatic moments in the UJA's forty-year history. Together with the results of the campaigns of 1975, 1976, and 1977, unsurpassed by any previous campaigns outside of the 1974 response to the Yom Kippur War, it defines the nature and quality of the Lautenberg years.

19.

The United Jewish Appeal at Forty

In the Bible, forty is both a precise number and a term used to indicate a long period of time. The years of the United Jewish Appeal, 1939–1978, are forty in number, but no four centuries can equal the historic turbulence of these eventful years. It was a time which witnessed the destruction of European Jewry and the rescue and rehabilitation of the surviving remnant; the fulfillment of a two-millennial dream in the founding of the State of Israel; the military, political, and economic battles waged by the fledgling state; its almost fivefold growth in its three decades; the *aliyah* of the Jewish communities of the Muslim countries of North Africa and the Near East; the unanticipated and continuing Jewish emigration from the Soviet Union; and the emergence of American Jewry into a united, affluent, influential community accepting the responsibility of leadership in world Jewry. In all of these the UJA and its beneficiary agencies played a central role.

We have noted and will later further define the work of the JDC and the United Israel Appeal/Jewish Agency in the great drama of a people resurrected. We must sum up the contribution of the UJA to the fashioning of the American Jewish community as we know it today. It provided both the motivation and the vehicle for uniting a community ready for unification. It forced campaigns unprecedented in scope on the individual communities, unearthing an unanticipated potential for philanthropy in the American Jew. The benefits from these campaigns, fueled by the impact of the United Jewish Appeal on the communities, were major and direct. Central communal campaigns raised $57.3 million in 1945; refugee plight raised the sum to $131.7 million in 1946, and the founding of the State of Israel to $205 million in 1948. The giving then decreased and leveled off, but never to a sum below more than twice that of the pre-1946 figure. Similarly, the Six-Day War raised the campaign results from $136 to $317 million; in the years following the average was well above twice the 1966 figure. The increase in the post–Yom Kippur War campaign was a $280 million jump to $660 million.

In the late 1960s and 1970s a substantial and increasing percentage of the total campaign remained in the community coffers, to be allocated to local, national, and overseas needs. The power to allocate is the power of influence and decision-making. The community used that power to shape the priorities of Jewish communal interests, and delegated power of influence and decision to its national body, the Council of Jewish Federations and Welfare Funds.

The local communities and the council also benefited from a cadre of young leaders, educated, trained, and motivated by the UJA, who took positions of leadership in all manner of communal enterprises. The council especially benefited from the great campaigns which the UJA motivated, because the council's income is derived from local federation dues, determined largely by the amounts raised by the total campaign, special emergency campaign funds included. The special emergency funds were largely responsible for the most generous campaign giving.

The Council of Jewish Federations represents the first "grass-roots" national American Jewish representative body. When it celebrates its jubilee year in 1982, it will be readily recognized for what it is. Its forthcoming reorganization will give it the boldness to proclaim what it has always been reluctant to state: that at long last, after 140 years of effort, American Jewry is an organized and unified community under the aegis of the Council of Jewish Federations. At that time and at this, due recognition must be accorded to the signal contribution of the UJA to the growth, development, and power of the CJF. That this be done, whether formally or functionally, is important not only so much for the record as for the proper perception of the source of the CJF's strength, historic and continuing.

A less tangible but nevertheless important contribution was the pioneering efforts of the UJA to unite and marshal for national Jewish communal enterprise two important molders of public opinion, the rabbinate and the Jewish academicians. The Rabbinic Cabinet (formerly the Rabbinical Advisory Council) affords one of the few opportunities for American rabbis of all religious groups to counsel and work together. The UJA Faculty Advisory Cabinet has coopted the vast Jewish intellectual talent on university faculties for Jewish causes. The imaginative work being done with both groups might well serve as a model for other national Jewish bodies on how to utilize these two rich resources. The 1973 crisis demonstrated their key position in the American Jewish and general community.

The UJA has also demonstrated the rich potential for leadership and philanthropy in the American Jewish woman. Organized in 1946 to maximize women's participation as individual contributors in the national campaign in the face of the desperate plight of Jewish displaced persons in postwar Europe, the UJA National Women's Division has grown from a small network of scattered units to several hundred active local units which currently raise about $70 million in the general campaign—seven times the sum achieved in 1946. The division accounts for 12–15 percent of the general campaign annually. In addition to its national, regional, and statewide fundraising activities among women, it provides an interregional leadership solicitation force, supplies speakers for community women's division meetings throughout the country, has an ongoing program of obtaining major gifts from women of independent means, offers a series of overseas missions for leadership, conducts a basic solicitor training program, and carries out a year-round series of regional events and institutes devoted to leadership development and educational activities.

The division has assumed a $50-million commitment over a five-year period to pay for the human support services in the Project Renewal program. This marked the culmination of more than thirty years' activity initiated by Reba G. Wadel and Adele Rosenwald Levy, and carried on with high dedication by leaders like Sara Goodman, Mathilda Brailove, Paulette Oppert Fink, Fannie Schaenen, Elaine Winik, and Sylvia Hassenfeld.

The general chairmen reflect the changes which have taken place not only in the UJA but in the general community as well. The first three—Morgenthau, Warburg, and Rosenwald—were "distinguished sons of distinguished fathers," a continuity of the *noblesse oblige* tradition of a German Jewish elite which stood above community, but served it with generosity and grace. Morris W. Berinstein, Philip M. Klutznick, Joseph Meyerhoff, Max M. Fisher, Edward Ginsberg, Paul Zuckerman, and Frank R. Lautenberg rose to national leadership through service and leadership in their respective local communities. Their successors, Leonard R. Strelitz, Irwin S. Field and Herschel W. Blumberg are products of the UJA.

Rising to prominence in Norfolk, Virginia, Strelitz was the UJA's first chairman from the South. His strength was said to be based on persistent and successful solicitation at the major gifts ($10,000 and over) level. His 1978 campaign strategy, stressing a strengthening of top-level fundraising, resulted in an increase in pledge totals.

Field, the architect of record campaigns in Los Angeles, is the first UJA chairman produced by a Far West community. Growing up in a Jewishly cultured and committed home in Detroit, he began his involvement with Jewish life as an original member of the first UJA Young Leadership Cabinet. The inspiration and training he received was put to use in Los Angeles, where he rose to the campaign chairmanship of America's second-largest Jewish community. From there it was a continuation and return to national UJA leadership. It is natural then that, teamed with Bernstein, also a UJA product skilled and schooled in community campaigning, his stress would be on the continuing coordination between UJA and local communities. Thus, in January of 1979 he announced as a basic campaign enterprise Dialogue '79, "a comprehensive program of in-depth consultations with a substantial number of communities during the period of February 26 to March 9":

> The agenda of each Dialogue '79 visit by a team of national and regional leaders, with professional support staff, will be tailored to the individual community's needs and campaign opportunities. . . . In addition . . . we plan to have lay and professional personnel available from our national divisions to meet with appropriate groups of women, young leaders, professional women, rabbis, faculty and students.

In its first forty years of existence, the UJA was allocated $4.9 billion from a total of $7.8 billion raised by central community campaigns. In addition, it obtained over $60 million for the Israel Education Fund, and helped create the atmosphere which made possible the sale of some $3.5 billion in State of Israel Bonds. The 1978 central communal campaigns raised $470 million, of which $278 million (or 61 percent) went to the UJA. The rest, $192 million, remained in the communities to be allocated by them for local and national needs.

That year also saw the launching of Project Renewal, "a sweeping social rehabilitation program for 300,000 people in Israel's distressed immigrant neighborhoods." The program aims beyond monetary contributions to direct cooperative involvement of American Jews in upgrading living conditions in Israel's most depressed neighborhoods and in the social and economic integration of their residents into the larger community. Its architects see it as a vehicle not only for revitalizing slum areas, but also for establishing a relationship between American Jewry and a sector of Israeli society of which it has little knowledge and with which it has even less contact. To this end, American communities are establishing linkages with specific neighborhoods. It is a bold and imaginative project, fraught with all the problems and dangers which serious and significant social engineering present. Its success will depend not so much on the funds raised, important as they are, but primarily on the skill, sensitivity, and patience of those charged with its implementation. A successful Project Renewal will not only accrue great benefits to the people of Israel, but will also have much of importance to say to other nations facing similar problems—the upgrading of the quality of life and the social integration of their submerged masses. Project Renewal presents to Israel and to world Jewry an opportunity to meet the challenge of Isaiah's vision of the Jewish people as a "light unto the nations," and of Herzl's description of a Jewish state in his Utopian *Altneuland*.

Despite the achievements of the UJA, this most remarkable of philanthropic endeavors, critical voices are heard regarding its impact on the economy of Israel and community life in the United States. Two such voices are those of serious and thoughtful Israelis. The *Jerusalem Post* of March 25–31, 1979, reported: "Abraham Shavit [chairman of the Israeli Manufacturers Association] called for a stop to the present system of UJA fund-raising, which tended to represent Israel as a poor and deprived society, which needed charity. 'The UJA raised $270 million for us last year, while exports brought $7 billion. The campaign does untold damage to the *Aliyah* efforts and to our efforts to sell sophisticated products abroad.' "

Shavit is a responsible and concerned person. He recognizes the good done by the monies raised, but he is critical of the manner in which they are raised. It would be well for the UJA to reconsider its campaign tactics which have served so well till now, in the light of new Israeli realities, and in consultation with leaders in the economic, intellectual, and academic sectors of Israeli society. Project Renewal, which points to the poverty pockets, a specific problem in the Israeli social system—but also a condition afflicting even the most affluent of nations—seems a step in the right direction.

The observation of Israeli political scientist and journalist Yosef Goell is more challenging. In an article in the April 22–28, 1979, issue of the *Jerusalem Post,* he argued that although the "financial contributions by American Jewry to Israel are important . . . they are less so than they used to be in the overall context of the Israeli economy." He also notes that the infusion of monies from abroad through donations "is undeniably inflationary," and that the easy access to such funds has "created a marked tendency among our political leaders to solve problems the easy way—by throwing American Jewish money at them." His criticism then is of the unwise, and at times undisciplined, use of these funds. It may well be that the donors do not exercise sufficient control over the use of their donations, but the forces which led to the reconstitution of the Jewish Agency in 1971 and the establishment of Project Renewal in 1978 seem well aware of the problem described by Dr. Goell. The outcome of Project Renewal will be a test of the validity of this observation and critique.

What is of greater consequence to American Jewry is a problem which, Goell claims, fundraising creates in the American Jewish community: "For American Jewry, the long-term and continuing Israeli emphasis on money donations has served to distort the terms of affiliation of many Jews with organized Jewish communities. The criterion of 'How much have you given?' has become so central, that many people have kept away from affiliation."

Goell may have used some journalistic license in overstating his case, but the issue he raises is one that the responsible leadership of the American Jewish community cannot afford to ignore. It touches upon two central problems confronting American Jewish life: the relationship between American Jewry and Israel, and the relationship between the individual American Jew and the organized Jewish community. Has the incessant emphasis on fundraising indeed relegated the relationship between the communities of America and Israel to that of donor-recipient? Is the place and worth of an American Jew within his community determined solely or largely by the size of his monetary contribution? Will American Jewry thus keep from active leadership some of its most thoughtful, creative, and committed men and women?

There is no question but that these issues must be confronted by an American Jewry now closely structured and formidably united. The most dramatic and forceful way for it to be placed on the agenda of American Jewish concern is to have it raised by the UJA itself, the organization which is held most responsible for creating the problem and which would be most affected by its resolution. It would need to do so in the context of the broadest gamut of organized Jewish enterprise, and in conjunction with the Council of Jewish Federations, which has become the functional representative of organized American Jewry.

The CJF has recently completed a self-study, a "Review of the Purpose, Function, Program and Organization of Council of Jewish Federations." In the course of the deliberations, there were those who perceived a trend toward the eventual incorporation of the UJA into the CJF. It was deemed necessary to issue this statement at the general assembly of the CJF on November 10, 1978: "Misconceptions have come to our attention concerning the draft report of the Review. It is not the intention to make the UJA a subservient organization of CJF. . . . It was never intended that the CJF usurp or take over the responsibilities of UJA."

The Board of Directors of the CJF, meeting on March 17–18, 1979, unanimously approved "Position Paper No. 7—CJF/Federation/UJA Relationships," to which a statement, jointly agreed upon by the CJF-UJA Joint Liaison Committee, was added. Its opening paragraph reads: "CJF recognizes the primary and central position that UJA carries in the annual national campaign. CJF recognizes further the enormous contributions UJA has made in strengthening American Jewish communities while carrying great responsibilities for overseas needs."

The statement calls for a "working partnership" between the two, which would utilize "the strengths of both autonomous organizations to meet common goals."

The April 1979 unpublished "Report on the Review . . ." notes: "UJA's important role in fund-raising is recognized . . . [and] substantial progress [has] already [been] achieved in joint planning and activities between UJA and CJF. It is recommended that other areas for such collaboration be explored."

The agreements arrived at by the CJF and UJA liaison committees provide for CJF representatives to serve on the UJA board, governance, budget and finance, and "other key committees." The UJA will also present its budget "to an appropriate CJF group of Federation leaders for review and advice." In return the UJA president and campaign chairman will serve on the CJF board. This seems to be a "logical step" in the direction of a formally structured and united Jewish community for which the UJA helped lay the foundation. But a caveat ought to be voiced, especially when we hear the suggestion that the next "logical step" should be toward the integration of the UJA into the CJF as its fundraising arm.

It is clear that in the past the sums raised by the local central communal campaigns were made possible by an independent UJA, which made campaign demands far in excess of what the federations would have wanted to undertake. It was able to get very large contributions, and raise these sums because of the donor's confidence that the sums he pledged would go most directly to the cause which inspired his donation. It is most reasonable to assume that in the future, a federation campaign no longer spurred by an independent UJA would lose far more than any gain which would be made by an "economy of operation." The losers in a diminished campaign would be not only the beneficiary agencies of the UJA, but also the local federations and the national and local causes which they support.

An independent UJA would also provide the organized Jewish community with a "fail-safe" vehicle for continued experimentation in the integration of special groups such as rabbis, academics, and women into the national Jewish communal enterprise, and their most effective utilization in the programs of that enterprise.

In considerations of the future place and role of the UJA in the American Jewish communal enterprise, it would be well to keep in mind this simple declarative statement about the UJA's forty years of life and accomplishment:

The United Jewish Appeal serves as the joint fundraising organization for its two corporate members: the JDC and the United Israel Appeal, Inc. (UIA).

The JDC is in its 66th year of providing rescue, relief and rehabilitation services for migrants and other Jews in need the world over; vital basic support for remnant Jewish communities in Europe, Asia and Africa, and innovative programming in Israel for the aging, the handicapped, underprivileged pre-school children and others.

The UIA, in its 55th year, channels funds received from UJA to the Jewish Agency for Israel, which provides a full range of services and programs—language and vocational training, housing, social welfare, rural settlement, youth care—all stemming from its primary concern for the movement, reception and absorption of immigrants from every corner of the earth. In addition, the support it provides to pre-school and higher education is crucial to the daily lives and future hopes of hundreds of thousands. In 1978, it added a Project Renewal Department. This department participates actively in comprehensive social and physical planning for the rehabilitation of distressed immigrant neighborhoods, disburses and monitors the use of funds, and evaluates implementation of the program.

With the funds distributed throughout its 40-year history, the UJA has contributed to the rescue and rehabilitation in free lands of well over three million men, women and children, about half of them immigrants brought to Israel.

This has been achieved through annual campaigns in American Jewish communities in all 50 states. There are currently 683

campaigning communities. Community campaign commitments to UJA during the 40 years have totaled $4.9 billion. This
represents 63 percent of the $7.8 billion pledged to community
campaigns since 1939.

The percentage of allocations to UJA has not been uniform
over the four decades. In the fluctuating pattern, four periods of
varying length are clearly definable.

1. During the war years of 1939 through 1944, community
campaigns raised a total of $194.9 million, of which the sum of
$92.1 million—or 47 percent—was allocated to UJA. With these
funds, UJA's agencies were able to rescue 162,000 Jews from
Hitler's Europe. Of that total, 76,000 were brought to Palestine
despite dangerous wartime conditions on land and sea; 86,000
reached other free countries.

2. In the post-war years of 1945 through 1947, when the
ghastly dimensions of the Holocaust and the desperate plight of
the survivors in the DP camps became painfully clear, new levels
in giving and allocations were attained. Out of community campaigns raising a total of $346.8 million, the sum of $248.2
million—or 72 percent—was allocated to UJA. UJA funds in this
period were used primarily to provide relief and welfare to more
than 250,000 displaced persons waiting on Cyprus, in Allied
Occupation Zone camps and in the rubble of their former homes
in Eastern Europe—waiting for the renewal beyond survival.

3. The 19-year period from the 1948 campaign, which hinged
on the creation of the new State of Israel, through the 1966
campaign was characterized by what has been called the greatest
homecoming in human history. The UJA, while helping to maintain remnant Jewish communities in Europe and Moslem countries through JDC, concentrated heavily on funding the absorption of more than a million immigrants it had helped bring to
Israel; in the process, UJA funds were largely responsible for the
creation of close to 500 agricultural settlements and more than
20 development towns. Allocated sums available during this
period totaled about $1.4 billion, or 55 percent of more than
$2.5 billion realized in community campaigns. In the 1966 cam-
paign, allocations actually dipped below the 50 percent mark.

4. The 12 campaigns, beginning with a 1967 campaign
spurred to new heights by the Six-Day War, continuing through
the quantum leap achieved in the 1974 campaign in response to
the Yom Kippur War, and concluding with the 1978 campaign,

realized the sum of slightly more than $4.7 billion. Allocations to UJA amounted to about $3.2 billion, representing approximately 67 percent of the total.

Most of the cash realized from these allocations during this period was applied by UJA to an intensified effort to provide full absorption services to new immigrants in Israel—including more than 130,000 Soviet Jews—and to several hundred thousand immigrants of prior years still not fully absorbed. The sums provided to the Jewish Agency, however, fell consistently short of its budgetary needs. The addition to the regular campaign in 1979 of Project Renewal represents an effort to make up for one crucial area of immigrant absorption neglect.

Alexis de Tocqueville observed that "as a general proposition . . . nothing is more opposed to the well-being of freedom of man than vast empires." He lauded the founding fathers of this republic for setting up a federal system which provided for a division of sovereignty, and accepted a multiplicity of loyalties. Others have pointed out that basic democracy in the United States is maintained by the acceptance of the legitimacy of a pluralistic society. It has also been argued that the strength of American Jewry lies in its pluralism, religious and cultural. It is pertinent, then, to suggest that as American Jewry becomes more formally united, attention should be directed to the preservation of its pluralistic character, "political" as well as religious and cultural. A system of checks and balances should be maintained or, if need be, established, lest an empire be fashioned which would lead to the detriment of the community and its individual members. An independent UJA would be able to serve as a vehicle for "checking and balancing," even as it is "checked and balanced."

In sum, just as the UJA in its first forty years made its signal contribution to the unity and strength of the American Jewish community, it can in its future decades continue to make its contribution beyond the needed dollars it raises. It can act as a testing organism for all manner of national Jewish activities and projects and it can help retain the pluralistic character of

American Jewry, a characteristic which has made that community unique and distinguished in the millennial Jewish communal experience.

In larger measure, it can make its contribution to America, as
it joins and gives direction to other Jewish groups in accepting
as a challenge the observation of American church historian
Winthrop S. Hudson:

> Perhaps one of the greatest contributions of Judaism to the
> United States will be to help other Americans understand how
> the United States can be a truly pluralistic society in which
> pluralism is maintained in a way that is enriching. . . . From the
> long experience of Judaism, Americans of other faiths can learn
> how this may be done with both grace and integrity.

Representative of the new generation of UJA leaders, who are
directing the UJA toward involvement in Jewish life beyond
fundraising, is its new national chairman, Herschel W. Blumberg. Raised in a religiously traditional, Zionist home in Baltimore, he received his Jewish education in Baltimore Hebrew
College, was a founding member of the UJA Young Leadership
Cabinet, and has served as president of the United Jewish Appeal Federation of Greater Washington, D.C., and of his
synagogue, Congregation B'nai Israel. He looks to an ever
closer working relationship between the UJA and the local
federations and toward an expansion of its involvement with
the synagogues and the national Jewish organizations. Participation in UJA activities he views as essentially a Jewish act, an
expression of one's Jewishness. "It's a Jewish organization, and
it must reflect the values and practices of Judaism—not just
because the chairman says so but because the leaders also want
it."

The new leadership is one with a commitment to Judaism
derived not so much from an inherited sense of duty, or from
nostalgia, as from knowledge and understanding. Their program for the UJA is aimed at the broadening of Jewish knowledge

which they are convinced will lead to an enlightened under-standing not only of Jewish needs but also of Jewish purpose. Only such knowledge and such understanding will result in the kind of commitment which will serve the UJA well. There is then, a tight congruence between UJA interests and intensive Jewish education and living. The role of Israel is central to the Jewish enterprise. Blumberg's view is unequivocal: "It's natural for me to believe in Israel—not just as haven, but also as a home for Jews from everywhere to live their lives." He looks to broaden the base of UJA participation not only because it will strengthen the campaign of the UJA, but also because it will intensify the Jewishness of the individual.

A community strengthened by the unity which the UJA has engendered and by the commitment which it is intensifying, can be the exemplar in America's pluralistic society of a group which will, in the words of Winthrop S. Hudson, "bear the burden of both commitments"—to America and to its heritage—and do so with "both grace and integrity." It will be the community which Israel Friedlaender envisioned in 1907:

> deeply rooted in the soil of Judaism, clinging to its past, working for its future. . . one in sentiment with their brethren wherever they are, attached to the land of their fathers. . . blending the best they possess with the best they encounter. . . adding a new note to the richness of American life, leading a new current into the stream of American civilization.

20.

This Spring in Jerusalem

This, the concluding chapter, is being written most appropriately in the city of Jerusalem. I sit at a table in the National Library at the Hebrew University surrounded by books and manuscripts important and fascinating to this student of history. But far more fascinating than the books found on the shelves are the books encountered on the street, in the home, in a store, in an office. The people of Jerusalem are living books. Each has his tale to tell, a tale fashioned by the most eventful forty years in the four thousand-year-old history of the Jewish people. Their cumulative biography is the history of our people in our time. It is the great epic of the twentieth century: destruction and death; rescue and rehabilitation; yearning and achievement. And as its climax, the triumphant tale of a people accepting destiny as duty to make its once and future homeland a safe haven and a secure home for the saved and saving remnant, and among them my Jerusalem friends, Hayim, Natan, Tsfirah, Avraham, David and German.

Hayim

The outbreak of the war in 1939 found Hayim Rosenthal in the Polish army. Born and raised in the small Polish town of Amdur

(Indura), he hoped from childhood to live and work in Palestine. In the difficult prewar months, he concluded that the only way he could get to this land of his dreams was through the Polish army. During the Nazi conquest of Poland he was wounded in battle, was captured, and spent two years in German prisoner-of-war camps, most of the time in the notorious Stalag Al.

In 1941 the Germans, preparing to attack their erstwhile Russian allies, decided to rid themselves of their wounded prisoners, and so permitted them to make their way home. Hayim's native town was then occupied by Soviet troops and he thought it too dangerous for a known Zionist to go there, so he made his way to Warsaw, arriving just in time to become a resident of its newly created ghetto. As a wounded veteran in Polish army uniform, he was able to get in and out of the ghetto, smuggling food and letters through the ghetto gates.

He remembers the rich cultural life in the ghetto: lectures, discussion groups, classes, concerts. Most vivid are his memories of participation in the underground resistance movement. He asks us to remember—to remember those who organized, trained, and disciplined themselves for the Uprising of the Warsaw Ghetto, to remember those who fought and those who fell. The Dror (Freedom) group of which he was a part smuggled him out of Warsaw to go to the ghettoes of smaller cities to organize youth resistance groups whose immediate duty would be to fight, but whose ultimate goal was to settle in kibbutzim in Palestine. His *shlihut* took him to Ostrowa and then to Czestochowa. Ghettoes closed him in, but he moved on. In 1943, he and a handful of colleagues, realizing that the ghettoes served only as the gathering places for the death factories, took to the forests.

For two years this first Jewish partisan band, never numbering more than fifty or sixty, carried on its activities of helping fellow Jews and fighting the enemy. They were hunted by Poles and Nazis alike, but Hayim recalls with satisfaction that they were able to send a few small groups of *halutzim* southward to Slovakia; some even reached Palestine.

In 1945 liberation came and the partisans set out at once to organize a center for the surviving remnant. Hayim was sent to travel through Poland to seek out survivors. He recalls:

> I found Jewish houses. I found Jewish furniture. But I found no Jews. Do you know what it is to come to a town which once throbbed with Jewish life, and not find a single solitary Jew? And when at long last I would come upon one or a few who somehow managed to survive, they were afraid to talk to me. They simply could no longer believe that there was anyone left in the world who cared about them, who would want to help them.

Two years in the stalags, two years in the ghettoes, and two years as a partisan in the forests were now followed by two years of organizing *Bricha*, the underground illegal immigration to Palestine. The money was supplied by the Joint Distribution Committee; the personnel came from the Yishuv in Palestine and survivors from ghettoes and death camps. In 1947, Hayim decided that his own lifelong yearning for life and labor in Palestine could no longer be postponed. As the head of a group of illegal immigrants on the small boat *Patras Panama*, he reached its shores just in time to join the Haganah and fight in the War of Independence.

The war over, the struggle for life began anew. The remnants of the death camps of Europe were flooding a country short on food, housing, and the network of health and social agencies which this immigration required. Hayim recalls life in the new state as very hard, but he and his fellow immigrants knew that they were welcome; fellow Jews abroad extended aid, and, as the rabbis observed, *"Tsarot rabim hatsi nehama*—trouble shared is half a consolation."

Hayim had prepared himself to come to the land *livnot, ul'hibanot bah*—to build and be rebuilt by it—so he went to work: in heavy construction; on guard duty; for the farm cooperative T'nuvah. In 1956, the Histadrut, observing his obvious leadership and organizational skills, invited him to work in its program of absorption and social integration of new immigrants.

Among the new immigrants of the latest wave was Sana Shapiro, a physician who arrived in 1972 with her father, mother, and daughter. Hayim and Sana married soon thereafter. Their three-and-a-half-year-old daughter Yifat is named after Hayim's remarkable sister, Priva, whose modest home in the Geulah section of Jerusalem was a veritable absorption center in miniature for many newcomers for whom it was a haven until they were able to find a home.

Natan

Shaomah, wife of Said Vahab, a carpenter of the city of Gariat al Gabel near Sana in Yemen, bore him nine children, of whom four survived childhood. Among these was Natan, who remembers the normal childhood of a boy of the ancient Jewish Yemenite community: close family life, an all-pervading piety, *heder* studies, and a love for and dreams of Zion.

He also remembers the anti-Jewish riots which greeted the establishment of the State of Israel, and the death of his parents. For orphans, there was danger of forcible conversion to Islam, so with a younger brother he joined a group of ten families of his town journeying to the Holy Land. A long, hard, dangerous trip to Aden "on roads which were not roads" was made possible through judicious bribery. In Aden they were received in an immigrant camp, and Natan remembers with gratitude the food, shelter, clothing, and medical care provided them by the Jewish Agency. Then from the skies came the planes of Operation Magic Carpet which lifted them to the Holy Land in 1949. He will also never forget the trauma of having his *peyot*, earlocks, cut off on the pretext of sanitary requirements. He has been able to channel his anger into constructive efforts for the preservation of Yemenite culture and piety.

In September 1949, his first home in Israel was in an abandoned military barracks in Rosh Ha-ayin. Then with *aliyat noar* to Natanya: "Fine food, good life, schooling . . . but a twelve-year-old in first grade." A knowledge of Hebrew and a natural ability quickly moved him on to Grade 6 and then to K'far ha-Noar Ha-dati, the Village of Religious Youth, near Haifa. There followed preparation for the army, army service, and settlement in the Lachish area in 1955, at the beginning of that imaginative experiment in social planning—a program of immigrant absorption which took due regard of the human, psychological needs of the immigrant. A central city, Kiryat Gat, where social integration took its natural course in school, the marketplace, and economic enterprises, was surrounded by ethnic villages where the new immigrants experienced the stability and psychological security of living with their own groups in their inherited cultural patterns.

The road to Jerusalem was long and circuitous for Natan, and the journey took twelve years, but it was accomplished in 1960. He became an iron worker to help build up the Holy City. He soon recognized that, as important as it was to build a city, it was more important still to give firm foundation and healthy structure to its people. He turned to youth work, becoming a most successful organizer of the Noar Dati, the Religious Youth Movement. Nor did he neglect the building of a family. Yona, of the family of Nadov who came in 1950 from the city of Manache in Yemen, and Natan were married in 1963. They live in the Bayit V'gan section of Jerusalem with their four daughters, Abigail, Tsofia, Hagit, and Yifat.

Natan, who serves as the secretary of the Jerusalem section of government employees, is vastly proud of his Yemenite heritage and the Yemenite Jews. "Israel has never seen a finer *aliyah*," he boasts; "no group loves the land more, and none work harder in its rebuilding." All who have seen the drama of *kibbutz goluyot*, the Ingathering of Exiles, and who have come to know the qualities and shortcomings of each group, would voice a grateful "Amen!" to Natan's proud boast.

Tsfirah

Tsfirah, too, came on the Magic Carpet in the same year as Natan. Ten sons born to Rowa, wife of Hayim Zahara in the town of Madar, Yemen, had died in infancy before Tsfirah's birth. In 1939, at the age of fourteen, she was given in marriage to a tanner and bore him a son and a daughter. Both father and husband were good providers and life was good.

"Why did we come to Israel?" she replied to my query, "All our lives we dreamed of the Land of Israel. 'V'hayta M'dinah, v'hayta aliyah—and there was a state, and there was aliyah.' " By foot and donkey the family traveled a whole month toward Aden. The city was filled with Jews awaiting emigration, so they had to camp on the roadside. Her husband died on the way, but with her six-year-old daughter and three-year-old son she pressed on. At last they boarded the plane which took them to Lod.

Their first home in Israel was in the tent city at Rosh Ha-ayin. Her father, who had come earlier, brought her and her children to Ein Shemen, a town of small huts, the ma'abarot. She recalls the hard days there, the sickness and the suffering. In Talpiot immigrant housing she remembers the crowded conditions, families sharing a single room.

Her father, who had been a businessman in Yemen, was now a common laborer, but he maintained with dignity the Yemenite patriarchal traditions. "He took care of everything," she stated simply. Remarried to a relative, she bore him three children, but he was a sickly and difficult person, and they went their separate ways.

As a widow, she was trained to be a cook and housekeeper, and now serves in that capacity at Bet Belgia, the Faculty Club at the Hebrew University. Her four children have all served in the army. The eldest, Yitzhak, works for the postal service and lives at home. "How can he get married," she explains, "when it is impossible to get an apartment?" Bracha is married to an English Jew who works at the port of Eilat. Herzl is a member of

Kibbutz Enat, and the youngest, Margalit, has just finished military service and is at home.

"They were ready to fight," she states, "and I am fighting too, fighting to get a better apartment," something larger than her two rooms which house three people. It has become her chief ambition, but she feels frustrated; "No one is helping me" is her sorrowful plaint. But as one hears it, one senses that she keeps repeating it not out of frustration, but in the hope that someone will listen. And the manner in which she states it seems to indicate that this daughter of a community so strong in faith has the faith that there are those who care and those who will be ready to help her now, as they have in the past.

Avraham

Avraham was the youngest of the five sons of Azar and Miriam Sellouk of Casablanca, Morocco. He was a child during the war years. He remembers planes rumbling overhead, and he remembers Arabs taunting Jews with "The Liberator is coming." The liberator whose coming they awaited was Adolf Hitler. He recalls attacks upon Jews, but does not forget the protection extended by the king of Morocco. As a youngster he heard his father tell of their family's origins in the Spanish city of Seluca, and of his ancestors' remaining strong in their faith in 1492, rejecting apostasy and choosing exile.

The family tradition of obstinate loyalty to faith and people took him after his bar mitzvah to *hachshara,* preparation for *aliyah* to the new State of Israel. An older brother had preceded him and settled in Ramlah. In January 1950, Avraham was one of a group of young people who came on *aliyat noar,* the youth immigration to Israel. Four and a half centuries earlier, his ancestors had fled from the country where once they lived in security and well-being, to a hostile backward land across the Mediterranean; now a descendant crossed the same ocean to be welcomed by a country created for him.

The Kibbutz Ramat Hashofet, named for Justice Louis D. Brandeis, was his home in 1953 and 1954. Then with a group of young pioneers from Egypt, Roumania, and Morocco he settled Kibbutz Merhavia. Three years of army service followed and then the kibbutz again. The rest of the family, his parents and two brothers, came in 1950 as part of the great Moroccan immigration, settling first in Ramlah and then in Jerusalem. The Sellouk family pilgrimage, which had begun centuries earlier, was completed when its youngest member Avraham settled in the Holy City. There he married Denise, whose family had come from Casablanca the same year as the Sellouks. They live with their four children, Miriam, Rachel, Dafna, and Moti, in the German Colony section of Jerusalem. Five centuries of wandering had come to an end.

David

It was only on the fourth attempt that David Hai Telzur was able to cross the border into Palestine. Even then he had to bribe the Jordanian gendarmes who had caught and imprisoned him.

He was born and raised in Baghdad, one of four sons of Tova and Yitzhak Telzor, a bookbinder. His early years in the 1920s and 1930s were uneventful, the usual growing up and schooling of an Iraqi Jew. He remembers, when he was a high schooler in 1941, the anti-Semitic spoutings of the grand mufti of Jerusalem, exiled by the British, then resident in Baghdad; the pro-Nazi uprising of Rashid Ali suppressed only after the British retook the city; and most of all, pogroms in Baghdad, with murder, pillage, and rape. He recalls the *kever achim,* "brothers' grave" of murdered Jews.

The hostility of the local population remained after the pogroms, and Iraqi Jews began to flee, some making their way to Palestine, whose gates were officially shut to Jewish immigration. In David's family and among his friends all thoughts turned to *aliyah.* He speaks with reverence and awe of the legendary Enzio Sereni, the emissary of Palestinian Jewry who with colleagues Ezra Khedouri and Shmaryahu Gutman taught Iraqi Jewish youth Hebrew and trained them for defense and *aliyah.* From Sereni, who died a hero's death as a parachutist on a mission of rescue to European Jewry, he heard of a "ghetto uprising in Europe."

David became a leader in the Iraqi underground, organizing *aliyah* to Palestine, a task fraught with mortal danger. In 1944, he decided to attempt *aliyah* himself. Dressed in Bedouin garb, he was able to reach the Iraqi-Syrian frontier, where he was caught and sent back to Baghdad to prison. On his release he returned to his studies and his underground activities, but he was now a marked man. His parents and two younger brothers, armed with false passports and posing as tourists, got to Syria, and then were able to make their way on foot to K'far Giladi. From there they continued on to Jerusalem.

His family in Palestine, David's obsession was to join them. With a group of like-minded young people he set out again, only to be thwarted by the *leil hagesharim,* the "night of the bridges," when the destruction of the bridges made entry into Palestine impossible. In 1947, again posing as a Bedouin, he set out with three companions. In northern Iraq they were caught. Four months of imprisonment and torture followed, and he was warned that if he tried again, he would not be returned alive.

His Hechalutz organization, working for his release, offered as surety for him a number of colleagues who themselves had made ready to flee the city. David refused the offer, was able to bribe his guards, and made his escape. A week later the underground was able to move him, hidden in a closed car, to the Jordan River, from which he set out for Kibbutz Bet Aravah. Jordanian police caught him, but a bribe secured his release, and on May 1, 1947, he reached the kibbutz. After visiting his family in Jerusalem he was off for Haganah military training in K'far Etzion, and played his part in the War of Independence.

Out of the army, he trained as a mechanic and worked in the Froumine bakeries, as a road builder, as a glazier, and for the municipality of Jerusalem. In that capacity he was able to welcome fellow Iraqi Jews who were brought in the great airlift appropriately named Operation Ezra-Nehemiah. In 1964 he married a Sabra, and they are the proud parents of a son and daughter, Elon Yitzhak, twelve, and Mihal, nine and a half.

German

A headline in the *New York Times* of October 26, 1976, read: "THIRTY JEWS IN MOSCOW SEIZED IN PROTEST." The story reported:

> About thirty Jewish activists were arrested today as the Soviet authorities moved to cut off further demonstrations by would-be emigrants. . . . The Jews spent five days at the Communist Party's Central Committee offices demanding written notification of how long they would have to wait to leave the country. . . . At the end of the day on Friday, they ignored orders to leave the Central Committee's reception room, and this violation was the reported basis for today's arrest. Among those seized were . . . Dr. German Shapiro, a Riga physician.

The name was well known to me. For four years, his family—father, mother, and sisters—who had reached Israel from Riga in that most unexpected and remarkable of *aliyot,* had been trying to pry him out of the Soviet Union, but to no avail. At their request, I spoke to a fellow Rochesterian, Kenneth Keating, United States ambassador to Israel, but he was powerless to help. Word came from Dr. Shapiro suggesting that I write to senators and congressmen and send copies of my letters and their replies to him. His expectation was that the Soviet authorities would intercept them, and thus become aware that members of the United States Congress were interested in his cause and concerned about his welfare. Those were the days of the Helsinki Agreement, when Soviet authorities were most sensitive to public opinion and congressional surveillance.

The letters were sent and replies from the senators and congressmen as well, but no word from Dr. Shapiro—silence from the land of the silent. But Dr. Shapiro was not among the silent.

Together with fellow "refuseniks" he protested, demonstrated, and continued to petition for reunion with his family and repatriation to his homeland—Israel.

It was only after he reached Israel early in 1977 that he wrote me: "I received not only your letters but also the copies of those written by senators and representatives . . . I sent you several letters from Russia before but I realize you did not receive them. The last . . . was taken from me when I was arrested and searched in Vilna, where I had gone to give a lecture on Jewish culture for refuseniks."

His efforts were rewarded with imprisonment in October 1976, which his wife learned of only from the radio. The Voice of America broadcast listed him among those who had been thrown into jail.

Early in December of that year he was informed by the Department of the Interior that his request had been granted, and that he had ten days to depart. The days stretched into a month, but with the new year the Shapiro family—Dr. German, Dr. Anna, Tanya, nineteen, and Michael, three and a half—began a new life in Israel.

The Shapiro family odyssey to Israel had begun forty years earlier. In 1939, the elder Dr. Shapiro, a physician in Riga, visited Palestine with a view to settling his family there. On his return he urged the entire Shapiro clan, over three hundred in number, to go on *aliyah*. But "cooler heads" prevailed. The family was a prominent one. Its members had carved out distinguished careers in the professions and in commerce. Why leave for a strange and distant land and an unknown future? By 1945 only thirty of the family were among the living. German's immediate family—father, mother, and two sisters—survived because during the war years Dr. Shapiro served as a physician in a military hospital in Orienburg, in the southern Urals.

The war over, they returned to Riga. As an "excellent" student, young German was admitted to the Riga Medical Institute. He recalls: "In 1952 when I entered the Institute, I was one of about one hundred Jews in a class of three hundred and fifty.

When my daughter was denied entry in 1976, the class of three hundred and fifty now numbered eleven Jews."

After medical school, Dr. German served for two years in a rural town in Latvia and from 1960 to 1972 he was on the staff of the prestigious Hospital of Biophysics of the USSR Ministry of Health, rising to the position of associate professor of endocrinology. In 1972 when he applied for an emigration visa he was immediately dismissed.

The decision to go to Israel had been some five years in the making. News of the Six-Day War aroused latent Jewish national sentiments in the hearts of many Russian Jews, the Shapiros included. In 1970, after the Leningrad and Riga trials, they began to talk seriously of *aliyah*. German's father, mother, two sisters, niece, and nephew were permitted to depart in 1972, and settled in Jerusalem. The four-year struggle of the German Shapiro family then began.

Denied an exit visa because of the "secrets he held," he petitioned again and again. He organized a seminar on Jewish culture in Riga, to which he had returned after his dismissal in Moscow, and lectured in other cities. He activated protests, formed and signed petitions, and carried on an ongoing duel with the KGB. During all that ordeal he was strengthened in his determination by the letters he received from his family telling of their reception and adjustment in Israel, and he was heartened by the knowledge that fellow Jews in the Free World stood ready to help him leave, get to Israel, and become established there.

He was able to thank all who helped him and his fellow Russian Jews at what the *New York Times* of May 2, 1977, headlined as "200,000 AT RALLY FOR SOVIET JEWS." The article reported:

One of the last speakers was German Shapiro, a Jewish physician, who was allowed to emigrate three months ago from Riga, Latvia, with his wife, who is a physician, and two children. They were permitted to go to Israel after four years. . . . Dr. Shapiro thanked Americans "who helped me to be free," but added: "I am here, but many are still prevented from leaving Russia. They are punished only for their desire to be Jewish and to raise their children as Jews."

From the window of their living room in the new neighborhood of Ramot, he has a view of the whole city of Jerusalem. With his wife, a doctor for Kupat Holim, daughter Tanya, a student in the Hadassah School of Nursing, and son Michael, a "star" of his Gan, we looked out one night at the twinkling lights of the city which once had been the goal of their odyssey, and now was their home. A Jew and his family had come home.

21.

Epilogue: On a Personal Note

I was one of nine cousins growing up in the Polish city of Grodno and town of Amdur in the 1920s and 1930s. Three of us are now alive: my cousin Pua in Israel, and my sister and I in the States. Two-thirds of my generation of the Karpowich and Schor families were murdered in their youth. I mourn their loss every day, but I will not surrender to despair. To surrender to despair would give ultimate victory to the Enemy.

Martin Buber's observation is an insight turned to mandate: "The prophet is appointed to oppose the King, and even more, history."

The Jewish people, "if not prophets, then the sons of prophets," have stood up to history once and again and again. We have refused to permit history to overwhelm us, to defeat us, even in our most fateful of generations.

Shlomo, Abrasha, Sarah, Sonia, Mimi, and Rachel live now only in memory. My cousins were taken from me. And I, the Jew, take to myself six others from that extended family called the Jewish people, and call them my cousins: Hayim, Natan, Tsfirah, Avraham, David, German.

May my cousins in unmarked graves in Poland rest in peace.

May my cousins alive in Jerusalem live in peace.

My story is the story of so many, many American Jews. We are crushed by the sorrow of such massive and cruel bereavement, but are able to rise above despair and to snatch victory from the teeth of the enemy, by joining together to give new hope and new life to those of our generation who had been denied it.

However much our exertion of heart and hand has done for them, it has done far more for us.

Many of us may have heard from their grandfathers, as I heard from mine, Reb Mattes, *zichrono Livracha:*

"To give life—is to live!"

Mishkenot Sha'ananim
Jerusalem, 1980

Bibliographical Notes

I. Toward Unity

1. *The Sense of Community*

For an account of American Jewry's response to the Damascus blood libel, see: Joseph L. Blau and Salo W. Baron, *The Jews in the United States 1790–1840* (New York, 1963), 3: 924–55; and Abraham J. Karp, *Beginnings, Early American Judaica* (Philadelphia, 1975), pp. 41–7. The latter also contains a facsimile reproduction of *Persecution of the Jews in the East* (Philadelphia, 1840), an account of the "Meeting of the Ismelites Resident in Philadelphia."

2. *A Community Organizes*

For the Cleveland Conference and reaction to it, see W. Gunther Plant, *The Growth of Reform Judaism* (New York, 1965), pp. 19–24.

The impact of the Mortara Affair on the Jews of America is fully described in Bertram W. Korn, *The American Reaction to the Mortara Case, 1858–1859* (Cincinnati, 1957). For the Board of Delegates of American Israelites, see: Allan Tarshish, "The Board of Delegates of American Israelites," *Publications of the American Jewish Historical Society (PAJHS)* 49, no. 1 (September 1959): 16–32; and Max J. Kohler, "The Board of Delegates of American Israelites, 1859–1878," *PAJHS* 29 (1925): 75–135, which contains important primary source material reproduced in the appendices.

3. *A Position of Parity*

Organized activities in behalf of the Russian Jewish emigrant by European Jewry are described by Mark Wischnitzer in his *To Dwell in Safety* (Philadelphia, 1948), pp. 37*ff.* Aid extended to the eastern European Jewish immigrants in America is delineated in Wischnitzer's *Visas to Freedom* (Cleveland and New York, 1950), pp. 27*ff;* and in Abraham J. Karp, *Golden Door to America* (New York, 1976), pp. 205–21.

4. *The Perception of Power*
The Yiddish original of the election handbill supporting Theodore Roosevelt is in the possession of the author.

American Intercession on Behalf of Jews in the Diplomatic Correspondence of the United States 1840–1938 by Cyrus Adler and Aaron Margolith, published as volume 36 of the *PAJHS* (Philadelphia, 1943), contains exhaustive documentation of the editors' claim "that Jews have been the chief beneficiaries of the humanitarian policies of the United States. . . . Whenever and wherever anti-Jewish feelings have expressed themselves in oppressive measures against Jews, the voice of outraged America was always raised in protest, and there were times when the American people, independently or through its elected governments, chose more specific action to communicate its disfavor. But it was necessary for American Jewry to call the oppressive measures to the attention of the American people and the American government and to urge the expression of outrage of the former and the intercession of the latter."

For reaction to the Kishinev Pogrom, see Cyrus Adler, ed., *The Voice of America on Kishineff* (Philadelphia, 1904).

For the history and activities of the American Jewish Committee, see: Naomi Wiener Cohen, *Not Free to Desist* (Philadelphia, 1972); and Nathan Schachner, *The Price of Liberty* (New York, 1948).

5. *Democracy from Above*
Full accounts of the American Jewish Congress and the American Jewish Conference are contained in unpublished doctoral dissertations (available from University Microfilms, Ann Arbor, Michigan): Morris Fromer, "The American Jewish Congress, A History 1914–1950" (1978); and Isaac Neustadt-Noy, "The Unending Task: Efforts to Unite American Jewry from the American Jewish Congress to the American Jewish Conference" (1976).

Both organizations issued numerous reports. Particularly noteworthy are the four volumes of *Proceedings* of the four sessions of the American Jewish Conference, 1944–1947, the first two edited by Alexander S. Kohanski and the latter two by Ruth Hershman.

II.   To Aid A Brother

6. *"That They May Not Hunger and Perish"*
For Karigal's mission to the New World, see: Stanley S. Chyet, *Carigal Preaches in Newport* (Cincinnati, 1966); and Karp, *Golden Door,* "Emissary from Hebron," pp. 11–17. Salo W. Baron and Jeanette Baron's *Palestinian*

Messengers in America (New York, 1943) deals with philanthropic activities by American Jewry on behalf of the Jews in Palestine in the nineteenth century. The letter of Sir Moses Montefiore is in the possession of the author. The poem by Saphir, "Gay Hizayon," was published in Jerusalem in 1856. The letters of solicitation of both the Board of Delegates and the Mikveh Israel Congregation are in the possession of the author. Rabbi Heller's report was published in the *American Jewish Year Book (AJYB)* (5664, 1903–1904), pp. 17–39. The quotations are found on pages 21 and 39.

Of books on American Jewish philanthropy, we call attention to the following:

Boris D. Bogen, *Jewish Philanthropy* (New York, 1917), is "a revision of a course of lectures on Jewish philanthropy given for the last six years at the Hebrew Union College of Cincinnati, Ohio."

Henry H. Rosenfelt, *This Thing of Giving* (New York, 1924), discusses "how sixty-three million dollars were raised in America to relieve the fear-stricken Jews of Europe and Palestine."

Milton Goldin, *Why They Give* (New York, 1976), is a popular, readable, and at times flippant account of "the politics, principles, and methods of money-raising in the world's richest Jewish Community," written by a "professional fund-raiser." It contains an extended and useful bibliography.

Marc Lee Raphael, ed., *Undertaking American Jewish Philanthropy* (New York, 1979), is a volume of informative reports, thoughtful essays, and critical evaluations of the philanthropic enterprise in the contemporary Jewish community.

7. *"Appeal to Their Brethren in America"*

Wertheim's letter appears in the "Eighth Annual Report of the American Jewish Committee," published in *AJYB* (5676, 1915–1916), pp. 360–63.

The response of the Orthodox Jewish community to overseas needs in World War I is documented in Morris Engelman, *Four Years of Relief and War Work by the Jews of America 1914–1918* (New York, 1918).

For the American Jewish Joint Distribution Committee, see: Joseph C. Hyman, "Twenty-five Years of American Aid to Jews Overseas: A Record of the JDC," *AJYB* (5700, 1939–1940), pp. 141–79; Oscar Handlin, *A Continuing Task, The American Jewish Joint Distribution Committee, 1914–1964* (New York, 1965); and Yehudah Bauer, *My Brother's Keeper: A History of the American Jewish Joint Distribution Committee, 1929–1939* (Philadelphia, 1974).

The work of the JDC was recorded in a number of reports, among them: *Reports Received by the Joint Distribution Committee of Funds for Jewish War Sufferers* (New York, 1916); and Dr. Boris D. Bogen, "Report of Joint Distribution Committee Activities in Poland" (February–June 1920).

8. *"Enduring Cooperation on Behalf of Jewish Causes"*

A *Report of Proceedings of the Preliminary Conference of the American Jewish Congress* (Philadelphia, March 27–28, 1916), was issued by the

Executive Organization Committee of the American Jewish Congress. It contains a detailed report of the organization of the congress, the chief addresses, and the purpose and membership of the committees.

Dr. Louis Rubinson, chairman of the Jewish Congress Committee of Philadelphia, in welcoming the delegates pointed to the appropriateness that "Here in this city of Brotherly Love, the Cradle of American Liberty, we have come together to plan ways and means of serving the oppressed—our unfortunate brethren in foreign lands—of obtaining for them the same degree of religious and civil freedom which we now enjoy in the United States." The democratic, folk character of the movement was dramatically expressed in the choice of the solicitor of financial contributions—Joseph Barondess, by then a legendary figure as an early heroic leader of Jewish labor on New York's Lower East Side.

For the tension and conflicts between Zionists and non-Zionists in the 1920s, and the establishment of the United Palestine Appeal, see Melvin I. Urofsky, *American Zionism from Herzl to the Holocaust* (New York, 1975), pp. 323*ff.* The Rosenwald statement is quoted on p. 324.

"The Report of the Joint Palestine Survey Commission" was first published in *New Judea* (London, June 29, 1928), and reprinted in *AJYB* (5689, 1928), pp. 55–70. The issuance of the report was followed by the Non-Zionist Conference Concerning Palestine, convened in New York on October 20–21, 1928, which resulted in the formation of the Jewish Agency. The *Proceedings of the Non-Zionist Conference Concerning Palestine* were published in pamphlet form as a verbatim report. The tenor of the meeting can be gauged from Felix A. Warburg's call: "It is hard to find a country that is so inspiring, that makes you do things . . . as does Palestine. . . . The people are worthwhile. The effort is worthwhile. . . . Every Jew in the United States should help that country stand on its own feet, and we should do it in a way that is most business-like, most painless for the recipients. And let us have as many players in the game and as few coaches on the sidelines as possible. (Applause)" (*Proceedings,* p. 21).

For an account of the joint campaign of 1929, see *AJYB* (5691, 1930), pp. 69–70; and *AJYB* (5692, 1931), pp. 29–30.

9. "A Lasting and Permanent Unity"

For the joint campaign, the United Jewish Appeal, in 1934–1935, and for the subsequent individual campaigns, see: *AJYB* (5696, 1936), pp. 212–13; and Bauer, *My Brother's Keeper,* pp. 166*ff.* The efforts of the Council of Jewish Federations and Welfare Funds to induce cooperation between the JDC and UPA are recorded in the *AJYB* (5697, 1937), pp. 243–44. See also Harry L. Lurie, *A Heritage Affirmed* (Philadelphia, 1961), p. 137.

For the founding of the United Jewish Appeal for Refugee and Overseas Needs, see: *AJYB* (5699, 1939), pp. 205–6; Lurie, *Heritage Affirmed,* p. 139*ff;* typescript in "The Story of the United Jewish Appeal, 1939–1963," anonymous archives of the United Jewish Appeal, New York, pp. 1–5;

and "Fourteen Years United Jewish Appeal," anonymous typescript in the archives of the UJA, New York, pp. 1–9.

The first public announcement of the establishment of the UJA was in a telegram sent by Edward M. M. Warburg, chairman of the Greater New York Campaign, to Abraham Landau, who presided at a testimonial dinner honoring Sidney Hillman, held at the Hotel Commodore, January 10, 1939, announced in the *New York Times,* January 11, 1939.

The agreement establishing the UJA was signed by Rabbi Jonah B. Wise representing the JDC, Rabbi Abba Hillel Silver representing the UPA, and William Rosenwald representing the National Coordinating Committee Fund. The organizational committee consisted of: (from the JDC): Paul Baerwald, Isidor Coons, Joseph C. Hyman, Henry Ittelson, Albert D. Lasker, Samuel D. Leidesdorf, Solomon Lowenstein, James N. Rosenberg, William Rosenwald, Edward M. M. Warburg, and Rabbi Jonah B. Wise; (from the UPA): Rabbi Israel Goldstein, Louis Lipsky, Henry Montor, Morris Rothenberg, Rabbi Abba Hillel Silver, and Rabbi Stephen S. Wise; (from the Council of Federations and Welfare Funds): Harry L. Lurie, Charles Rosenbloom, William J. Schroeder, Joseph Willen, and Ira Younker.

III. We Are One

10. *The United Jewish Appeal: Beginnings*

The "Review of the Year" which appeared in the annual *American Jewish Year Book,* contained concise, authoritative reports on what was happening in the major Jewish communities of the world. The *Year Book* is a particularly good source for activities within the organized Jewish community in America. An *Index to Volumes 1–50* (1899–1949, 5660–5709), was prepared by Elfrida C. Solis-Cohen and published by KTAV Publishing House (New York, 1967).

The United Jewish Appeal maintains meticulously organized archives, and is engaged in an ongoing Oral History Project, which is recording interviews with major figures in UJA history and modern and contemporary Jewish life. Both the archives and the Oral History Project are rich repositories of primary source material indispensable to the student of contemporary Jewish life.

The opening quote is from the introduction to "Part I: The United States" of "Review of the Year 5700," *AJYB* (5701, 1940), pp. 269–70.

The Silver-Wise statement is quoted from *AJYB* (5701, 1941), p. 95.

The Ginzberg volume was published by Harper and Brothers (New York, 1942).

The views of the American Jewish Committee were expressed in a draft prepared by a subcommittee headed by Louis E. Kirstein, appointed "to achieve a common statement of principles to which all Jewish organizations would subscribe." The subcommittee felt it necessary first to formulate a statement on Palestine to which the American Jewish Committee could subscribe. *AJYB* (5704, 1943), pp. 211–12. For Zionist reaction, see *ibid.,* pp. 212–13.

The Franklin D. Roosevelt quote is cited in *AJYB* (5703, 1943), p. 199.

The articles of Geraldine Rosenfield on "Overseas Relief and Rehabilitation" in the *AJYB* for 5705, 5706, and 5707 (1944–1947), based on information supplied by the UJA, the JDC, HIAS, ORT, OSE, and the Vaad Hatzala, contain much of the pertinent data for this period.

The Schwartz statement is from "The United Jewish Appeal—1939–1955," typescript in the UJA archives, p. 4.

11.   1946: A Year of Testing and Triumph

For the national conference in Atlantic City, see: Geraldine Rosenfield, "Overseas Relief and Rehabilitation," *AJYB* (5706, 1946), pp. 202–3; Schwartz, "United Jewish Appeal," p. 5; interview of Henry Montor, 8/3/78, UJA Oral History, pp. 3*ff*; interview of Henry Montor (by author), 1/29/79 in Jerusalem; interview of Sam Abramson, 6/9/1977, UJA Oral History, pp. 12*ff*; interview of William Rosenwald, 3/13/1975, UJA Oral History.

For the Baron quote see Salo W. Baron, "The Year in Retrospect," *AJYB* (5708, 1947), p. 115.

12.   Eyes Toward Zion

For a report on the 1949 campaign, the UJA relationship with the communities, and precampaign budgeting, see *AJYB* (1951), pp. 125–27.

The Montor interviews cited above contain data and views on UJA–local communities confrontations.

The text of *A Resolution Adopted by Members of the American Delegation at the Jerusalem Conference* and a list of the delegates was published by the UJA in the fall of 1950.

13.   1947–1950: Years of Rescue and Return

For Morgenthau, see *Encyclopedia Judaica,* 12: 321–22.

The interview with Dr. Israel Goldstein (4/6/75), UJA Oral History Project, pp. 22*ff*, contains an evaluation and appreciation of Morgenthau, the man and the UJA leader.

For Montor, see: *Encyclopedia Judaica,* 12: 281; interview with Israel Goldstein, cited above, pp. 40–41: "Montor is a dominant personality . . . brilliant . . . resourceful . . . his insistence that we were underestimating the capacity of the American Jewish community to contribute . . . proved to be right."

14.   In and with the Communities

Reference to the Spektor responsum (originally published in *Yerushalayim* vol. IX, 1911 ed., Abraham Luncz, p. 49), is found in Baron and Baron, *Palestinian Messengers,* p. 266 n. 85.

For Schwartz, see *Encyclopedia Judaica* 14: 1020; his "The United Jewish Appeal—1939–1955"; and his address at the National Inaugural Conference of the UJA, Miami Beach, February 15, 1953, "Time Lost Now May Mean Lives Lost Later," published by the UJA.

For Edward M.M. Warburg, see *Encyclopedia Judaica* 16: 285. The Warburg address to the annual national conference was published by the UJA.

15. At the Tercentenary and Beyond

For a report and analysis of the campaigns of 1945 through 1953, see *AJYB* (1955), pp. 253–57.

In the report on "Jewish Communal Services" in the *AJYB* (1956), it is stated: "Successive annual declines in campaign results brought the 1954 campaign total to $107.5 million. Because of the rise in the price level of about 50 percent since 1945, the purchasing power of pledges in 1954 was approximately equal to that of 1945, the last year prior to the postwar emergency period. . . . 89 percent of the amounts raised was provided by 17 percent of the contributors. The average per capita gift . . . was $29.70. . . . the average per capita gift to community chests . . . was $4.37" (p. 228).

The survivor poster and similar campaign posters and literature which were provided by the UJA to local welfare fund campaigns are preserved in the archives of the UJA.

16. Confrontation and Cooperation

For William Rosenwald, see *Encyclopedia Judaica* 14: 298–99. Appreciation for his role in the UJA is found in the UJA Oral History Project interviews of Pinhas Sapir (n.d.), p. 7; Philip Klutznick (March 1976), p. 26; and Israel Goldstein (4/6/75), pp. 11–12.

For Herbert A. Friedman, see: *Encyclopedia Judaica* 7: 186; interview with Friedman (4/27/76), UJA Oral History Project. The author is grateful to Marc Tabatchnik, Henry Montor, Sam Abramson, and Irving Bernstein for data and evaluation of the role of Friedman in his professional leadership of UJA.

For UJA–Council of Jewish Federations and Welfare Funds confrontation and cooperation, see UJA Oral History Project interviews with Friedman (4/27/76) and Philip Bernstein (3/21/76).

The Stock analysis is found in his "The Reconstitution of the Jewish Agency: A Political Analysis," *AJYB* (1952), pp. 178–93.

17. Leadership from the Community

For historical background on the period under discussion, see Abraham J. Karp, "American Jewry 1954–1971," in Rufus Learsi, ed., *The Jews in America* (New York: KTAV, 1972), pp. 359–98.

Interview with Joseph Meyerhoff (9/9/75), UJA Oral History Project.

For Meyerhoff, see *Encyclopedia Judaica* 11: 1468; for Fisher, see *Encyclopedia Judaica* 6: 1330.

The Fisher address was published by the Reform Jewish Appeal.

18. *The Summer of 1967 and the Fall of 1973*

For campaign results, see annual reports in *AJYB*. The UJA archives contain complete records of the campaigns.

The quote is from Karp, "American Jewry," p. 373.

Interview with Philip Bernstein, (3/21/76), UJA Dial History Project.

Ernest Stock, "Reconstitution," points out: "In 1966, the net amount made available to the Jewish Agency from worldwide campaigns was $60 million; in 1967, it was $346 million" (p. 187).

The Ginsberg, Zuckerman, and Lautenberg addresses, in typescript, are in the UJA archives.

The Elazar study is Appendix A in his *Community and Polity* (Philadelphia, 1976), pp. 341–77.

19. *The United Jewish Appeal at Forty*

This summary chapter is based on data heretofore cited or described in the text.

Winthrop S. Hudson, *Religion in America* (New York, 1973), pp. 440–41.

Israel Friedlaender, *Past and Present* (Cincinnati, 1919), p. 278.

20. *This Spring in Jerusalem*

The interviews were conducted by the author in Jerusalem in the spring of 1979. He is grateful to Hayim Rosenthal for his help.

Index

Abramson, Sam, 89
Academicians in fundraising, 161,
   163, 168
Adler, Cyrus, 26, 28
Agro–Joint, 61–63
Agudas Harabonim, 47–48
Alexander II (czar), 15
Aliyah. See Immigration to Israel
Alliance Israelite, 16, 42
Allied Jewish Campaign, 63, 65–66
Altneuland (Herzl), 164
American Committee for
   Ameliorating the Condition of the
   Russian Refugees, 17, 20; *An
   Appeal,* 17
American Council for Judaism, 34,
   80, 84
American Financial and
   Development Corporation for
   Israel, 97
American Hebrew Congregations,
   Union of, 12, 20, 48
American Jewish Assembly, 80
American Jewish Committee,
   31–35, 69, 141; activities of,
   28–29, 35, 45–46, 48, 59–60, 80;

influence of, 29, 128; Ninth
   Annual Report, 26, 28
American Jewish Congress, 31–33,
   59–60
American Jewish Joint Agricultural
   Corporation (Agro-Joint), 61–63
American Jewish Relief Committee,
   49, 60
American Jewish Year Book, 26,
   107, 126
American Jewry as world leaders,
   43, 77, 159
American Palestine Campaign,
   67–68. *See also* United Palestine
   Appeal
American Relief Society for Indigent
   Jews in Jerusalem, Palestine, 40,
   42
American Zionists, Federation of,
   46, 48
Anti-Semitism, 12, 24, 29, 138–39,
   180–81, 183–84; blood libel, 3,
   26; burning of synagogues,
   70–71; the Holocaust, 34, 77, 85,
   120, 154; the Inquisition, 23;
   pogroms, 15, 25–26, 42–43, 56,

Anti-Semitism, (Continued)
70, 180; Pope Pius IX, 10; riots in
Palestine, 63, 66; the Warsaw
Ghetto, 174–75
Arbeiter Ring, 48
Assimilation of immigrants, 72,
111, 114–15, 163–64, 176–77
Associated Jewish Charities, 139
Association for New Americans, of
New York, 115
Atlantic City, N.J., 87–89

Baeck, Leo, 154, 156
Balfour Declaration, 32, 61
Baltimore, Md., 139
Baron, Salo, 90
Baron de Hirsch Fund, 17
Ben-Gurion, David, 96–97, 115,
128
Berinstein, Morris W., 138, 162
Bernstein, Irving, 150, 152, 154
Bernstein, Philip, 129, 147, 152
Bible, 118, 120, 159, 164
Blaustein, Jacob, 128
Blumberg, Herschel W., 171–72
B'nai B'rith, Independent Order of,
20
Board of Delegates of American
Israelites, 11, 16, 42
Board of Deputies, Jewish, 4
Bonds for Israel, 97, 100, 126.
See also, State of Israel Bonds
Brailove, Mathilda, 162
Brandeis, Louis D., 49, 59, 63, 66,
179; and Kibbutz Ramat
Hashofet, 179
Brown, David A., 61, 106
Bureau of Jewish Social Research,
69

Capouchin, Thomas, 3
Central Committee for Relief of the
Jews Suffering Through the War,
47–50

Central Committee of Palestine
Institutions, 47
Central Refugee Committee, 17
Charity, Jewish. *See* Philanthropy,
Jewish
Charleston, S.C., 6
Chasseaud, Jasper, 3
Chicago, Ill., 96, 115
Children, care of, 124, 176–77; in
orphanages, 42; in schools, 40,
42, 109–10, 140, 146
Cleveland, Ohio, 9, 150
Community Chest, United States,
114
Community federations. *See* Local
federations
Congregations. *See* Synagogues
Conservative United Synagogues of
America, 48
Coons, Isidor, 88
Council of all Kolelim in New York,
109
Council of Jewish Federations and
Welfare Funds (CJF), 84, 90;
increasing importance of, 68–70,
127–29, 160–61; and the Large
City Budgeting Council, 70; and
the United Jewish Appeal, 141,
143, 147–48, 152, 166–67
Crémieux, Isaac, 4
Crisis philanthropy, 42–43, 117,
145–47, 160–61; pogroms in
Germany, 70–71; pogroms in the
Soviet Union (Russia) 16, 20;
riots in Palestine, 63–64, 66–67;
Six-Day War, 145–47; World
War I, 45–50; World War II, 77,
85, 87; Yom Kippur War, 151–54
Critics of aid to Israel, 164–66

Damascus Affair, 3–4, 6–7, 14, 21,
24
Das Judisches Hilfskomite für Polen,
50

De Tocqueville, Alexis, 170
Detroit, Mich., 150
Dinitz, Simcha, ix, 150
Discord among American Jews, 7,
    9–10, 20–21, 62–64, 127, 132.
    See also German Jews versus
    Eastern European Jews; Zionists
    versus non-Zionists
Displaced persons. *See* Immigration
Diversity, of·American Jews, reasons
    for preserving, 170–71
Drachman, Bernard, 47

Einhorn, David, 9–10
Elazar, Daniel J., 152–54; and "The
    American Jewish Response to the
    Yom Kippur War," 152–53; and
    "The Advantages of
    Organization," 153
Elchanan Spektor, Isaac, 109
Elitism, in Jewish relief leadership,
    28–29, 31, 60, 137, 162
Ellinger, Moritz, 16
Emergency Rescue Fund, 126,
    145–47, 160. *See also* Special
    Funds
Emigration from: Arab countries,
    111; Europe, 117, 124, 175;
    Germany, 9; Iraq, 180–82;
    Morocco, 42, 124, 179–80;
    North Africa, 117, 124; Poland,
    175; the Soviet Union (Russia),
    15–16, 20, 42, 151, 182–85; the
    United States, 149–50; Yemen,
    118, 120, 176–78
Enlarged Jewish Agency, 66

Faculty Advisory Cabinet, 161
Federation of Jewish Philanthropies,
    106
Field, Irwin S., x, 131, 162–63
Finance. *See* Fundraising
Fink, Paulette Oppert, 162
Fischel, Harry, 49

Fisher, Max M., 129, 141–43,
    147–48, 162; and the American
    Judaism Award of the Reform
    Jewish Appeal, 142
Forsyth, John, 3
Frankel, Lee K., 62
Free Sons of Israel, 20
Friedlaender, Israel, 172
Friedman, Herbert A., 121, 125–27,
    129–30, 132, 134, 147–50
Fundraising: academicians in, 161,
    163; and the role of education,
    109–10, 129–30, 135, 150,
    153–54; and the role of
    organization, 152–54; rabbis in,
    132, 134, 161, 163; and special
    funds, 126, 134, 140–41,
    145–47; women in, 134, 161–63.
    See also Fundraising, decreases in;
    Fundraising, methods of;
    Fundraising, statistics of;
    Philanthropy, Jewish
Fundraising, by Israeli (Palestinian)
    emissaries, 39–40, 96–97, 100,
    115
Fundraising, decreases in, 90, 107,
    111, 117–18, 125–26, 160
Fundraising, methods of, 93, 106,
    109, 132, 146–47, 163; through
    literature, 120–21; missions to
    Israel, 131, 134–35, 162; open
    rallies, 152, precampaign
    pledging, 88–89, 106; soliciting
    major donors, 118, 152–53, 162;
    War Relief Stamps and
    Certificates, 50
Fundraising statistics, 49–50,
    56–57, 67, 71, 117, 142; of the
    Allied Jewish Campaign, 65–66;
    of the American Jewish
    Committee, 45–46; of the
    American Jewish Relief
    Committee, 49–50, 56–57; of the
    Joint Distribution Committee,

Fundraising Statistics, (Continued)
61–63, 70; of the United Jewish
Appeal *(1939-1957)*, 78, 84–85,
89, 111, 114–15, 126; of the
United Jewish Appeal
(1965-1978), 145–47, 152–54,
160–64
Funds, allocation of, 78–80; to the
Israel Education Fund, 146; to the
Joint Distribution Committee,
49–50, 68, 78, 84–85, 88, 93; to
local communities, 111–12, 118;
to the National Refugee Service,
78, 84; to the United Jewish
Appeal, 93, 118, 126; to the
United Palestine Appeal, 68, 78,
84, 88, 93
Funds, distribution of: to Central
and South America, 85; to
Europe, 42–43, 50, 57, 61–63,
85, 175; to the Middle East, 85;
to the United States, 16, 20, 42
Funds for Israel (Palestine), 39–40,
45–47, 109, 176; from the Joint
Distribution Committee, 50, 62;
from the United Jewish Appeal,
126, 146–47, 150, 152–53,
162–65

German Central Committee, 16
German Jews versus Eastern
European Jews, 15–16, 20–21,
25, 28, 59, 139
Ginsberg, Edward, 147–50, 156,
162
Ginsberg, Eli, 79
Glazenbrook, Otis A., 50
Goell, Yosef, 165–66
Goldman, Julius, 17
Goldstein, Israel, 100, 123–24
Goodman, Sara, 162
Gruber, Ruth, 118, 120
Guggenheim family, 26
Gutman, Shmaryahu, 180

Harrison, Earl G., 87; and the
Harrison Report, 87
Hassenfeld, Sylvia, 162
Hebrew Charities, United, 17
Hebrew Emigrant Aid Society, 16
Hebrew University (New York), 154
Heller, Maximillian, 42
Helsinki Agreement, 182
Herzl, Theodor, 164; *Altneuland*,
164
Heyman, Moses, 40
Hitler, Adolf, 67, 179
Holocaust, 34, 77, 85, 120, 154
Hoover, Herbert, 57
Hudson, Winthrop S., 171–72
Hull, Cordell, 99
Hyman, Moses, 40
Hyman, Solomon, 40

Immigrants, aid to: in Israel
(Palestine), 40, 42–43, 163–64,
175; in the United States, 16, 20
Immigration to Israel (Palestine),
114–15, 146; from Arab
countries, 111; from Europe, 85,
117; from Iraq, 180–82; from
Morocco, 124, 179–80; from
North Africa, 117, 124; from
Poland, 175; from the Soviet
Union (Russia), 151, 182–85;
from the United States, 149–50;
from Yemen, 118, 120, 176–78
Immigration to the United States, 9,
15, 16, 20, 42, 72
Institute on Overseas Studies, 128
Integration of immigrants, 72, 111,
114–15, 163–64, 176–77
Intergovernmental Committee on
Refugees, 87
Isaacs, Samuel M., 11, 42
Israel, State of, 80, 93; Jewish right
to, 32; need for, 36, 61, 112,
120–21, 151, 176; shift in
importance, 101, 106, 114

Israel Bonds Organization, 97, 115
Israel Education Fund (IEF), 146, 163
Israelite, 9
Israelitische Allianz aus Wien, 50

Jacob, Joseph, 21
Jacobs, Joseph, 4
Jerusalem Post, 164, 165
Jewish Agency, 63, 85, 129, 135, 159; reconstruction of, 148, 165
Jewish Agency for Palestine, 63
Jewish Alliance of America, 20
Jewish Board of Deputies, 4
Jewish Committee for Relief of Sufferers from the War, 50
Jewish commonwealth. See *Israel,* State of
Jewish Immigrants of Philadelphia, Association of, 20
Jewish Labor Committee, 34, 80
Jewish Members of the Repubican State Committee (New York), 23
Jewish Messenger, 11, 42
Jewish Publication Society, 12
Jewish Theological Seminary, 20
Joint Distribution Committee (JDC), 49–50, 78, 84, 88, 93; and aid to Europe, 60–63, 67–68, 85, 175; and aid to Israel (Palestine), 63, 85, 159; and the United Jewish Appeal, 70–72, 99, 115
Joint Palestine Survey Commission, 62

Kantrowitz, Jeruham Zvi, 109
Karigal, Isaac Haijm, 39
Keating, Kenneth, 182
Khedouri, Ezra, 180
Klutznick, Philip M., 138, 162
Kraus, Adolf, 26

Labor Committee, Jewish, 34, 80
Lautenberg, Frank R., 156–57, 162

Leeser, Isaac, 6–7, 9–10, 40, 42
Lehman, Herbert, 63
Levy, Adele Rosenwald, 162
Lewisohn family, 26
Local communities, 40; influence of, 118, 121, 160; needs of, 111, 131–32, and the United Jewish Appeal, 110, 125–27, 129, 140–41, 163. *See also* Local federations
Local federations: and local congregations, 132, 134; power of, 69–70, 79, 89–90, 111, 141; role of, 68–70, 73, 93, 96, 153; and the United Jewish Appeal, 127–29, 132, 134–35, 141–43, 147, 166–67
London, Meyer, 49
London Manor House Committee, 16
Look, 118, 120
Los Angeles, Calif., 140

Mack, Julian W., 49, 63
Magnes, Judah, 31, 50
Maimonides College, 12
Malki, Moses, 39
Marshall, Louis, 33, 61–63, 66; and the American Jewish Committee, 26, 28, 31, 45–49
Mayer Wise, Isaac, 9–10
Meir, Golda, 100
Melchett, Alfred Moritz Mond, 62
Meyerhoff, Joseph, 138–41, 162
Mikveh Israel congregation, Philadelphia, 6–7
Missions to Israel, 139–40, 146, 150, 162; rabbinic missions, 132, 134–35; This Year in Jerusalem, 156–57; Young Leadership missions, 131
Mizrachi, 47
Monsky, Henry, 34, 80
Montefiore, Moses, 4, 10, 40

Montor, Henry, 88–90, 96–97, 99–101, 106–07, 110
Morgenthau, Henry, Jr., 89, 97, 99–101, 137–38, 162
Morgenthau, Henry, Sr., 45–46, 138
Mortara, Edgardo, 10–11
Mortara Affair, 10–11, 14, 21, 24

Napoleon II, 10
National Conference for Jewish Communal Service, 69
National Conference of Jewish Charities, 69
National Coordinating Committee Fund, 71
National Refugee Service (NRS), 78, 84, 99, 123
National Women's Division of the United Jewish Appeal, 134, 161–62
Nazism, 33, 70–71, 77, 85, 120. See also Holocaust
Netkin, Nathan Neta, 39–40
Newport, R.I., 39
New York, N.Y., 4, 6–7, 10, 21, 23–24, 50
New York Association for New Americans, 115
New York Times, 182, 184–85
Nobless oblige, tradition of. See Philanthropy, Jewish, tradition of

Occident, 9, 42
Operation Ezra-Nehemiah, 182
Operation Magic Carpet, 120, 176, 178
Oppert Fink, Paulette, 162
Oppression, of Jews. See Anti-Semitism
Orphanages, 42
Orthodox Jews, 21, 47–48
Orthodox Jewish Congregations, Union of, 47–48

Palestine Economic Corporation, 63
Parity, of American Jewry with European Jewry, 17, 21, 56
Pennsylvania Inquirer and Daily Courier, 6
People's Relief Committee, 49–50
Persecution of Jews. See Anti-Semitism
Philadelphia, Pa., 6–7, 20, 32, 60
Philanthropy, Jewish: as a measure of Jewishness, 142, 165–66; philosophy of, 17, 64, 115, 125, 156; potential of, 79, 106–7, 118, 126, 160; in praise of, 57, 142; tradition of, 17, 162. See also Crisis Philanthropy
Pincus, Louis, 128–29
Pittsburgh, Pa., 20
Pius IX (pope), 10
Pogroms, 15, 25–26, 42–43, 56, 70, 180
Political persuasion, by American Jews, 12, 23–24, 26, 29, 151; Damascus Affair, 4, 6–7, 24; Mortara Affair, 10–11, 24; treaty with Switzerland, 10, 24; in the United Nations, 156; in World War II, 85, 99–100
Political persuasion, by European Jews: 4, 10, 15–16
Project Renewal, 162–65
Publication Society, Jewish, 12

Rabbinical Advisory Cabinet, 132, 134, 161
Rabbinic Cabinet, 132, 134, 161
Rabbis in fundraising, 132, 134, 161, 163
Red Cross, American, 50, 114
Reform Central Conference of American Rabbis, 48
Reform Congregations, Union of, 12
Reform Jews, 9–10, 11–12, 20, 80

Refugees. *See* Immigration
Refuseniks, 183
Republican State Committee, Jewish Members of (New York), 23
Rescue, of persecuted Jews, 16, 85, 99, 151
Resettlement of immigrants. *See* Immigrants, aid to
Richmond, Va., 6
Rights, Jewish, 9–10, 32–33, 61, 80
Rochester, N.Y., 109
Rockefeller, John D. Jr., 63
Roosevelt, Franklin Delano, 84, 99
Roosevelt, Theodore, 23, 26
Rosenberg, James, 62
Rosenblatt, Yosele, 50
Rosenthal, Hayim, 173–76
Rosenwald, Julius, 50, 61, 63, 89, 138
Rosenwald, Lessing, 84, 124
Rosenwald, William, 84, 88–89, 121, 123–25, 137–38, 162; and Kfar Rosenwald, 124
Rosenwald Levy, Adele, 162
Rothschild, Guy de, ix
Rothschild family, in Europe, 4
Ruppin, Arthur, 46
Russian Emigrant Relief Fund, 16
Russian Transportation Fund, 17

San Francisco, Calif., 10
Saphir, Jacob, 40
Sapir, Pinhas, 125, 152
Schaenen, Fannie, 162
Schiff, Jacob H., 26, 45–46, 48, 61, 112, 138
Schools, 40, 42, 109–10, 140, 146
Schwartz, Joseph J., 85, 110–11, 114–15, 125, 127
Selig, Aaron, 39
Sellouk, Avraham, 173, 179–80
Sereni, Enzio, 180–81
Shaarey Tefillah congregation, New York, 11

Shapiro, German, 173, 182–85
Shavit, Abraham, 164
Shearith Israel congregation, New York, 7
Sher, Zev, 152
Silver, Hillel, 71, 78
Sinai, 9
Six-Day War, 134, 145, 149, 160, 184
Solicitation. *See* Fundraising, methods of
Special Funds, 126, 134, 140–41. *See also* Emergency Rescue Fund
Spektor, Isaac Elchanan, 109
State of Israel Bonds, 146, 163. *See also* Bonds for Israel
Stock, Ernest, 129
Straus, Nathan, 45, 49–50, 60
Straus, Oscar, 26, 49
Strelitz, Leonard R., 162
Sulzberger, Mayer, 26, 28
Synagogues, role of, 48, 70–71

Telzur, David Hai, 173, 180–82
Terumat Ha-Kodesh, 40
Tocqueville, Alexis de, 170
Touro, Judah, 40; and Mishkenot Shaananim, 40
This Year in Jerusalem, 156–57. *See also,* Missions to Israel
Traditional Jews, 9–12, 20
Truman, Harry S., 87

Union of American Hebrew Congregations, 12, 20, 48
Union of Orthodox Jewish Congregations, 47–48
Union of Reform Congregations, 12
United Hebrew Charities, 17
United Israel Appeal, 115, 141, 159. *See also,* Jewish Agency
United Jewish Appeal (UJA): and allocation of funds, 93, 118, 126–27, 169–70; beginnings, 64,

United Jewish Appeal, (Continued)
67, 71–73, 78; and emergency
funds, 126, 145–47, 160; Faculty
Advisory Cabinet, 161; hegemony
of, 99; and the international
conference on the Holocaust,
154; and the Israel Education
Fund, 146, 163; and local
federations, 127–29, 132,
134–35, 141–43, 147, 166–67;
Missions to Israel, 131, 139–40,
146, 150, 156–57, 162; Project
Renewal, 162–65; Rabbinic
Cabinet, 132, 134, 161; and the
Six-Day War, 145–47, 149; and
statistics of fundraising
(1939–1957), 78, 84–85, 89, 111,
114–15, 126; and statistics of
fundraising *(1965–1978),*
145–47, 152–54, 160–64; in
summary, 168–70; and the United
Jewish Appeal National
Conference, 149; Women's
Division, 134, 161–62; and
World War II, 84–85; and the
Yom Kippur War, 150–53, 157;
Young Leadership Cabinet,
129–31, 134, 160–63, 171
United Jewish Campaign, 62
United Jewish Charities of
Rochester, 15
United Palestine Appeal (UPA), 62,
68, 70–71, 99, 101; allocation of
funds to, 68, 78, 84, 88, 93. *See
also,* American Palestinian
Campaign
United States Government, role of,
57, 182
United States relief agencies, 57
Unity, Jewish, 36, 72–73, 139, 149,
156, 170; and the Holocaust, 34,
67; in response to persecution, 4,
6–7, 11–12, 14, 26, 66; and
World War I, 47, 50

Urofsky, Melvin, 154; *We Are One,*
154

Vahab, Natan, 173, 176–77
Van Buren, Martin, 4, 6
Voice of America, 183

Wadel, Reba G., 162
Warburg, Edward M. M., 112, 114,
125, 137–38, 162
Warburg, Felix M., 48–49, 61–63,
112, 138
War of Independence, 175, 181
War Refugee Board, 99
War victims, aid to, 57
Wasserman, Oscar, 62
We Are One (Urofsky), 154
Welfare funds. *See* Local federations
Wertheim, Maurice, 45–46
Wiesel, Eli, 75
Willen, Joseph, 106
Wilowsky, Jacob David, 109
Wilson, Woodrow, 50
Winik, Elaine, 162
Wise, Isaac Mayer, 9–10
Wise, Jonah B., 71, 78
Wise, Stephen S., 33, 59–60
Wolf, Simon, 24
Women in fundraising, 100, 134,
161–63, 168
Women's National Division, of the
United Jewish Appeal, 134,
161–62

Yishuv, 47, 61, 175
Yom Kippur War, 139, 150–53, 157
Young Leadership Cabinet, 129–31,
134, 160–63, 171
Youth, care of. *See* Children, care of

Zahara, Tsfirah, 173, 178–79
Zionists, Federation of American,
46, 48

Zionists versus non-Zionists, 61–63, 65–66, 80, 84, 101, 123–24; and the American Jewish Congress, 31–33, 59–60; and the Rosenwalds, 123–24

Zuckerman, Paul, 150–51, 156, 162